Folk Britain

A Guide for Modern Times

Tom Howells

Contents

Introduction 6
A Note on Travel and Logistics 11
The Folk Calendar 12

Spring 23

Olney Pancake Race 24
Alnwick Shrovetide Football Match 26
Whuppity Scoorie 28
Jethart Hand Ba' 28
British and World Marbles Championship 30
Easter Monday Lifting 30
World Coal Carrying Championships 31
Marsden Cuckoo Day 31
Hare Pie Scramble and Bottle Kicking 32
Pace Egging Plays 34
Hungerford Hocktide 36
Beltane Fire Festival 38
Padstow Obby Oss 40
Hastings Jack in the Green 44
Blackawton International Festival of Worm Charming 46
Oxford University Tortoise Race 48
Ely Eel Day 49
Randwick Wap 49
Helston Flora Day 50
Whitby Penny Hedge 52
Tissington Well Dressing 54
Beating the Bounds 56

High Wycombe Mayor Weigh-In 58
Cooper's Hill Cheese-Rolling 60
Tetbury Woolsack Races 64
Bampton Morris Dance 66
The Hunting of the Earl of Rone 68
Robert Dover's Olimpick Games 70
Castleton Garland Day 72
Great Wishford's Oak Apple Day 74
Antient Scorton Silver Arrow 76
Maldon Mud Race 76

Summer 79

Hawick Common Riding 80
Mayor of Ock Street 84
Appleby Horse Fair 86
Glastonbury Festival 86
Summer Solstice 88
World Nettle Eating Championship 92
Whalton Baal Fire 94
Sma' Shot Day 96
Grasmere Rushbearing 98
World Peashooting Championship 100
Swan Upping 102
Moulton Crow Fair 106
Berwick Curfew Run 107
St Wilfrid's Feast Procession 107
Bread Ahead Lammas Day 108
National Eisteddfod of Wales 110
Mary Gibson's Mausoleum Inspection 112
Burning of Bartle 113
The Burryman Procession 114

Kettlewell Scarecrow Festival 116
Cilgerran Coracle Races 117
St Bartholomew's Bun Race 117
Knighthood of the Old Green 118
Kilwinning Papingo Shoot 120
Aberaeron Mackerel Fiesta 122
Birnam World Haggis-Eating Championship 124
World Bog Snorkelling Championships 124
Bramble Bank Cricket Match 126

Autumn 129

Crying the Neck 130
Throwing the Feat Stone 131
Braemar Highland Gathering 132
Colne Oyster Fisheries Opening Ceremony 134
World Stone Skimming Championships 134
Sowerby Bridge Rushbearing 136
Marldon Apple Pie Fair 138
Abbots Bromley Horn Dance 140
Egremont Crab Fair 142
Braughing Old Man's Day 144
Punkie Night 146
Samhain and Halloween 148
Lewes Bonfire 150
Ottery St Mary Tar Barrels 154
Turning the Stone 156
London Pickle Festival 158
Ackworth Harvest Sheaf 159
St Martin's Fair and Mock Mayor 159
Eton Wall Game 160

Winter...... 163

Holy Thorn Cutting...... 164
Montol...... 166
Tom Bawcock's Eve...... 170
Ringing the Devil's Knell...... 172
Newburgh Oddfellows Parade...... 173
Kirkwall Ba'...... 174
Old Time Paper Boys...... 177
Sword Dancing...... 180
Wassailing...... 182
Stromness Yule Log Pull...... 186
Allendale Tar Bar'l...... 187
Twelfth Night...... 190
Haxey Hood...... 194
Burning the Ashen Faggot...... 198
Selkirk Haggis Hunt...... 199
Burning of the Clavie...... 200
Whittlesea Straw Bear Festival...... 202
Chepstow Wassail and Mari Lwyd...... 204
Up Helly Aa...... 206
Marsden Imbolc Fire Festival...... 210
Hunting the Mallard...... 212
Calan Hen...... 212
Grimaldi Clown Service...... 213
Slaithwaite Moonraking...... 213
Hurling the Silver Ball...... 214
Boar's Head Ceremony...... 216

Further Resources...... 218
Events by Region...... 222

Introduction

Welcome, armchair traveller, to *Folk Britain: A Guide for Modern Times* – a pocket companion to the most weird, wonderful and profound cultural events this (mostly) green and pleasant land has to offer. Across the following pages, you'll find over 100 arcane rituals, historical reenactments, feats of sporting heroism, amateur dramatics, floriferous dances, eyebrow-singeing fire action, errant Osses and more Morris troupes than you can shake a coppiced stick at.

The disparate details of these centuries-spanning curiosities will be explained within – but it's helpful to get to grips with a few fundamentals before dusting off your peashooter.

What do we mean by 'folk culture'?

Though many rituals and events have their origins in distant history (several in this book are thought to have loose pagan origins, for instance), 'folk' does not necessarily mean archaic. Nor does it have to be connected to nature, although it is often synonymous with the rural or bucolic.

So, what the heck is it, then? In short, folk culture relates to the customs, practices and traditional beliefs of a particular community, expressed in highly localised and self-reflective ways. Folk culture has a symbiotic relationship with the location (a village or town, say) in which it emerges, and is performed and perpetuated by the people of that locale (the 'folk' themselves). Many folk customs – such as wassailing (p.182 and p.204), Morris dancing (p.66

and p.84) and mummers' plays (p.177) – are ubiquitous across wider regions, retaining shared themes and imagery but with their own unique or local twists.

Why these folky events?

There are hundreds of folk events across the calendar. The assortment we've chosen includes the largest and most iconic gatherings across the gamut of seasonal themes, as well as the dinkier, less showy and more obscure events, plus many others that simply tickled us. Crucially, they're all still active and very much living traditions.

Any regular communal event with esoteric or intimate significance to the participants is fit for the draw. This includes the relatively recent: events revived after many fallow years, such as the irreverent Stromness Yule Log Pull (p.186), or perhaps relatively new, as with the Blackawton International Festival of Worm Charming (p.46). Although they seem utterly crackers today, other events have been passed down through the generations and often reflect societal conventions of bygone days – whether celebrating the end of the harvest (such as Cornwall's Crying the Neck, p.130), commemorating a healthy fishing yield (see Tom Bawcock's Eve, p.170) or giving the finger to local authority (as in Lewes's insane and anarchic bonfire night, p.150).

These varied folk happenings are often imbued with an idiosyncratic oddness. From the timeworn and commemorative to the newfangled and wilfully lightweight, there's a very British element to proceedings, which chimes with our Monty Python-esque eccentricity and delight in playing even the weirdest situation straight.

Who can take part?

Many have hereditary or hyper-specific criteria for participation – such as the Abbots Bromley Horn Dance (p.140) or the election of the Mayor of Ock Street (p.84) – but welcome the presence of spectators. Fascinating curios, they provide snapshots of ages past, encouraging shared experiences quite removed from the trappings of modernity. Others are more liberal and encourage all to participate; perhaps after reading this book you might fancy your chances at shin-kicking (at Robert Dover's Olimpick Games, p.70) or cheese-rolling (at Cooper's Hill, p.60).

How did these events come about?

It's crucial to stress that, while the devil is usually in the details – very literally here, as several of the happenings gathered in this book feature some kind of lyrical interjection from Satan himself – the origins of many of these events are terribly vague. The question of 'who really knows?' is a consistent trope (particularly in the more ancient traditions, such as Shebbear's Turning the Stone, p.156). Try not to sweat the details and just enjoy the ride (perhaps via rushcart, as per p.136).

Why care about folk culture nowadays?

British folk culture was, for many recent decades, considered rather fusty. This is no longer the case. As attested by the contemporary boom in nature writing and rise of eco-activism, people wish to reconnect with their communities and reassess their relationship with the land. The ascendant embrace of folk reflects, perhaps, a desire for reprieve from modern life, simultaneously keeping alive the customs of our forebears. Plus, who doesn't fancy a perplexingly violent game of mob football to blow the cobwebs out (at the Kirkwall Ba', say, p.174)?

Now, folk culture is palpably present in everything from the hip cache of folksy zines like *Weird Walk* to the mainstream appeal of TV shows such as *Myth Country* – presented by Charlie Cooper of *This Country* fame, whose character, Kurtan, sums things up perfectly: 'That's the beautiful thing about living in the village. Everyone comes together on days like Scarecrow Festival and just forgets their utter hatred of each other.' (For a fuller account of related scarecrow festivities, see p.116.)

I'm hooked! How can I dive deeper?

Slightly further off the beaten track, folk culture is the subject of books like *The Lost Folk* by Lally MacBeth and *Finding Albion*, Zakia Sewell's decolonial delve into British folk zones. Visually, it is explored by illustrator Ben Edge, in his *Frontline Folklore* and *Children of Albion* series; and by performance artists like Lucy Wright (who enacts more inclusive folk practices, riffing on rushbearing or recasting iconic folk figures, as with her *Burry Woman*, a female version of Scotland's eerie bobble-covered Burryman) and Seamas Carey (with his raucous *Pagan Pandemonium* games). The music, film and fashion industries are also reflecting this growing interest in folk culture, for instance through the programming of London's Offbeat Folk Film Club, the independent Circle Dance record label and the appeal of folkloric motif-emblazoned tees from trendy designer brand, Heresy.

All this is to say that folk, in whichever form it may take, means as much to us now as it ever has – both in its jolly whimsy and surreal leanings, but more importantly as a means of reigniting a communal spark and engagement with our surroundings, in a world rent apart by the alienating forces of unfettered capitalism, online nihilism and outsider politics. At its heart, the folkloric year affords a magical, mystifying, microcosmic window into the past and present of our collective cultures – and what could be more stirring than that?

A Note on Travel and Logistics

As with the origins of these folky occurrences, the timings and locations are a tad hazy and subject to change. We therefore haven't provided much info on the practicalities of getting there – or how to get home after imbibing a bowl of steaming cider (at the Chepstow Wassail and parade of the Mari Lwyd, p.204, for example). To those ends, do check each gathering's website or socials for the latest intel, not least as the larger ones may have specific information on parking and road closures. Since many of these events are organised around religious days – the dates of which change each year – or need to occur on specific weekdays, they tend to slightly differ annually. It's worth checking the date before firmly committing; the website calendarcustoms.com is a fantastic resource for annually updated information on even the smallest ritual events, so should be a first stop.

The Folk Calendar

With its abundance of religious days, shifting New Year's dates, sprawling origin stories and key celestial touchpoints, the folk year is somewhat knotty. This book follows a seasonal structure, though it's helpful to understand the four Gaelic points of seasonal transition (otherwise known as the Wheel of the Year).

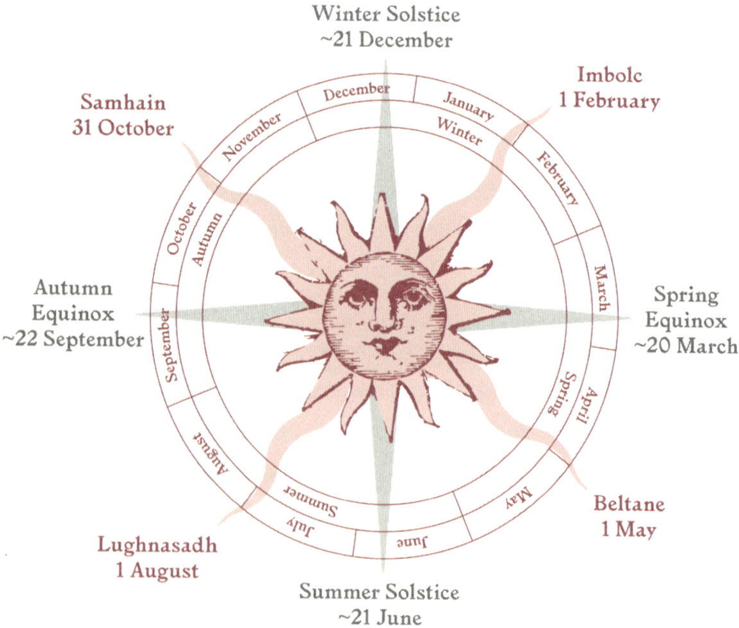

Imbolc

The Celtic arrival of spring is celebrated smack bang in the middle of the winter solstice and spring equinox – and is synonymous with the feast day of St Brigid, one of Ireland's patron saints. The name Imbolc derives from the Old Irish for 'in the belly', reflecting its themes of purification and fecundity, as the biting winter months begin to thaw out and ewes are readied for milking.

Beltane

Commemorated halfway between the spring equinox and summer solstice, this was the traditional Celtic inauguration of summer: a time of resurgent fertility when cattle could be put out to pasture in great shifts of herds and flocks, marked by raging bonfires and slap-up feasts.

Lughnasadh

The smell of freshly baked bread heralds the start of the harvest season, halfway between the summer solstice and autumn equinox. Dinners and dedications of the sun god Lugh were de rigueur, and the year's first sheaves of wheat would be cut, milled and baked into loaves – something synonymous with its Christianised English counterpart Lammas.

Samhain

This transition from autumn to winter opens the door to the incoming dark half of the year, a time for near crossover between the human and supernatural realms. It was observed with yet more fires to ward off spirits, plus feasts and fortune-telling divination.

Beltane (p.13) celebrations in Glastonbury, heralding the arrival of spring

The Hobby Horse and the Fool perform at The Hunting of the Earl of Rone (p.68), an annual village event unique to Combe Martin, Devon

The rugby-like Eton Wall Game (*p.160*)*, played at the boys' boarding school since 1776*

Above: Triangle playing at the Abbots Bromley Horn Dance (p.140)
Right: Flora and foliage abound at Jack in the Green festivities (p.44)

Spring

The transition from winter's gloom to the sun-dappled days of spring means celebrations across the land. The season's more alfresco appeal prompts various eccentric outdoor action: from the ruggedly physical to more genteel and quirky face-offs. Meanwhile, nature's newly budding greenery and vivid floral palettes are put to fine use in oversized garlands, Green Man adornments and well decorations; while Easter, Ascension Day and May's bank holidays see many jolly shindigs and traditional reenactments.

Olney Pancake Race

Flipping good footrace with a transatlantic twist

There is no more idyllic Easter pastime than a pancake race – and the village of Olney both invented *and* perpetuates it in its purest form. In this ladies-only race, competitors – who must be over 18 and have lived or worked in Olney for at least three months – run 380 metres from the Bull Hotel to the church, flipping a pancake at both the start and end. Contenders must bring their own pancakes (but aprons, pans and headscarves are provided).

It's believed that, back in the early 1400s, a busy housewife was making pancakes when the shriving bell was rung to summon people to the church of St Paul's. Flustered, she legged it – still holding her pan with 'cake in situ. Thus, the race was born and has continued since, lapsing before World War II but revived in 1948 by Rev. Ronald Collins. Charmingly, a civic organisation in Liberal, Kansas, got wind of things in 1950, challenging the folk of Olney to a transatlantic contest that goes on to this day, with times officiated via video link. At the time of writing, Liberal have won 42 races to Olney's 32. Galling!

Olney, Buckinghamshire, England
Shrove Tuesday

FRANCIS JACKSON
HOMES

Alnwick Shrovetide Football Match

Bushy football goals in the shadow of a duke's abode

The sopping Pastures below Alnwick Castle play host to one of the country's few surviving Shrove Tuesday football games – first recorded in 1762, but likely older (and its vague genesis thought to be in an affray between the Northumbrians and Scots).

A ball is brought to the meadow from the castle, in a procession led by the resident Duke of Northumberland's piper. Two teams of indeterminately massive size kick it between 1.2-metre-wide goals, known as 'hales', topped with bushy arches and set 402 metres apart. The team to score twice wins. The ball is then lobbed into the River Aln; whoever dives in and transports it to the river's far bank gets to keep it.

Sixty-odd years ago, the match was still played in the town, but vandalism like the smashing of windows meant it was banned, at which point the Duke instigated a revival on his own lands. For years, it was played between the parishioners of St Michael's and St Paul's, but these days anyone can partake – and be in with a chance of bagging £30 for scoring the winning hale.

Alnwick, Northumberland, England

Shrove Tuesday

Whuppity Scoorie

In this sweet seasonal segue, which begins when the bell at St Nicholas's rings for 6pm, scores of village children leg it clockwise around the church three times, swinging balls of paper on long strings around their heads to chase away evil spirits. It was first formally recorded in 1893, but is thought to have earlier etymological origins of a more masochistic kind, with pious locals being penitently 'whupped' around the church and then 'scoored' (or washed) in the river.

Lanark, South Lanarkshire, Scotland
1 March

Jethart Hand Ba'

This chaotic mob football match sees umpteen residents from either end of Jedburgh attempt to throw, carry or smuggle a stitched leather ball, either over an underground stream or across a set of railings – all in the hope of scoring the single winning goal. It starts at 2pm and goes on for hours. First recorded in 1704, it has been cancelled exactly once in its history, for Queen Victoria's funeral. The ball is said to symbolise the decapitated head of an Englishman: the attached ribbons his tousled locks.

Jedburgh, Scottish Borders, Scotland
Thursday after Shrove Tuesday (though varies)

The stitched leather ball fought over in the Jethart Hand Ba'

British and World Marbles Championship

It's teeny glass orbs at dawn in the world's foremost marble contest, staged at the Greyhound pub since 1932. Teams from as far afield as Japan and the USA have competed to knock their adversary's balls out of a sand-covered ring in the quickest time possible – the swiftest ever clearance a cool two minutes and 56 seconds in 1987, officiated by BBC's Record Breakers. The event harks back to a 16th-century contest between love rivals, who settled on marbles to win the heart of a local milkmaid.

Tinsley Green, West Sussex, England
Good Friday

Easter Monday Lifting

Mild vertigo sufferers beware: each Easter, the Blackheath Morris Men (formed in the 1960s and once banned from more southeast London pubs than any other folk dance group) usher in springtime with this uplifting custom. After performing a customary jig, they raise receptive ladies to shoulder height in a flower-covered chair, spinning it round three times. Traditionally, there's a 'reward' of a kiss – which may explain why the church used to frown on what was a more widespread affair in the 18th and 19th centuries, when it was known as 'heaving'.

Greenwich, London, England
Easter Monday

World Coal Carrying Championships

More macho posturing, this time in a former colliery hub. In 1963, Reggie Sedgewick and Amos Clapham were boozing at an inn when a third man, Lewis Hartley, popped in and joked how worn out Reggie looked. Perturbed, he suggested a race to the nearby green carrying a 50-kilogram sack of coal. It's now a staple: a 1-kilometre dart from the Royal Oak pub to Maypole Green, which a palpably coal-loving man called Andrew Corrigan has won each of the seven years in which he's raced. Women, meanwhile, are only obliged to carry 20 kilograms of the black stuff, and children (the idlers) race without any coal at all.

Gawthorpe, West Yorkshire, England
Easter Monday

Marsden Cuckoo Day

The appearance of cuckoos once announced the arrival of spring – a season the denizens of Marsden tried to render eternal by building a wall around one unfortunate bird, which escaped before they could lay the final brick. For the past two decades, the village has commemorated this with a charming festival and 'grand cuckoo procession', in which a huge cuckoo model is pulled through the streets on wheels, or sometimes held aloft and animated with a flapping mechanism. The spectacle is great fun (or terrifying, if you're an ornithophobe).

Marsden, West Yorkshire, England
Last Saturday in April

Hare Pie Scramble and Bottle Kicking

Sacred pastry and flying beer barrels in Leicestershire

It's two oddball customs for the price of one in Hallaton: one 'gastronomic' and one 'barbaric', according to a 1978 BBC TV programme. First, the Hare Pie Scramble. Channelling the archaic Christian 'dole' of food to parishioners, a sizeable pie is baked to a secret recipe. It's now made of beef, as hares aren't in season, but the long-eared bounder has remained in name, possibly due to its sacred status at Easter. This is blessed by the vicar of St Michael's and carried to a hill called Hare Pie Bank, then chopped up and thrown to the greedy throngs. What's left is popped in a sack and paraded to a field alongside three small wooden barrels filled with beer, known as the 'bottles'.

These become the focus of a sporting match between the residents of Hallaton and Medbourne. One is thrown in the air thrice; when it lands, the masses must transport it to the 'goals' of two streams, a mile apart, in a rule-free, bloody-nosed maraud across the fields. The second bottle follows suit and, if it's a tie, the third is heaved up as the decider.

Hallaton, Leicestershire, England
Easter Monday

Pace Egging Plays

An ovoid take on the traditional 'combat play'

A corruption of the Latin *pascha* for Easter, 'pace egging' comprises a splendid array of eggy occurrences around the north of England and bits of Scotland – from dyeing eggshells (with scraps like onion skins) to egg rolling – possibly dating back to the Crusades. All swell, but we're talking plays: specifically, the iconic combat play, in which a saintly or royal hero faces off against a villain. Combat plays are the most common form of mummers' play – roving, seasonal performances staged by am-dram troupes across the country. They are typically associated with Christmas-time, though in Cumbria, Lancashire and Yorkshire they are also performed at Easter.

The performance involves the King or St George taking on the Bold Slasher (or other adversary), alongside other characters including the improbably named Toss-Pot, a jovial tramp who goads the crowd with a pin-filled straw tail and demands gifts (like eggs). There are many beloved iterations: not least those at Heptonstall – led by a sword juggler – and Midgley, performed by the drama-loving teens of Calder High School since 1932.

Heptonstall and Midgley, Calderdale, West Yorkshire, England

Around Easter

Hungerford Hocktide

Technicolour 'Tutti Men' and a surplus of citrus

'Hocktide' is technically the Monday and Tuesday of the second week after Easter, the name possibly a derivation of the Saxon 'heah-tid', or 'high festival'. In Hungerford, it's celebrated over a fortnight, with a madcap array of folksy happenings particularly clustered around the Tuesday (known as Tutti Day). It's all a bit complex, so pay attention.

At 8am, a bell is rung and a hunting horn blown at the town hall, summoning the commoners. Soon thereafter, a Hocktide Court is gathered to discuss local business and elect specific officers, known collectively as the Hocktide Jury, and which includes a Constable, Water Bailiffs, Ale-testers and the Tutti Men.

The latter group, wearing top hats, are presented with floral, beribboned staffs before setting off down the high street with the Orangemen – a gang of orange-carrying subordinates who demand coins from the men and kisses from the women in exchange for oranges. The random inclusion of this fruit is a historical reference of support for William of Orange, who settled the terms of his royal ascendance at the town's Bear Hotel in 1688. Progress is invariably slowed by a variety of lubricating pub stops along the way.

Back at the Court, 'fines' are paid to preserve the common rights of grazing and fishing – originally granted by John of Gaunt to Hungerford's common folk way back in 1365, though the charter is long lost – and a Steward of the Manor reads a set of Ancient Customs, handed down from 1583.

There's then a four-course, speech-heavy lunch at the Corn Exchange (for which anyone can purchase a ticket), followed by an arcane custom called Shoeing the Colt, which sees a newcomer to the town (the 'Colt') being manhandled by the Official Blacksmith, who hammers a nail into their shoe until they cry 'Punch!' It's all very maniacal, with music and merriment lasting well into the evening – the Tutti Men and Orangemen stumbling back to the Three Swans Hotel for 9pm to return their staffs. Best see it for yourself.

Hungerford, Berkshire, England
Two weeks in April and specifically the second Tuesday after Easter

Beltane Fire Festival

Celtic-themed chaos overlooking Auld Reekie

One of the four seasonal Celtic transitions, Beltane marks the blazing, fertile return of summer. This commemorative event on Calton Hill is a modern iteration of the ancient Gaelic festival – founded in 1988 with support from Edinburgh University's School of Scottish Studies, it now boasts a 300-strong army of volunteers, arranging a ticketed, multifaceted celebration of the pastoral cycle.

At sundown, a procession headed by a May Queen and Green Man begins at the National Monument and loops anticlockwise around the hill. There's no denying the effort that's gone into the costumes and vibrantly painted personalities of the groups they 'awaken' along the way: crawling cats and woodland creatures, red-cloaked fire-spinners, Celts in white face paint, acrobatic figures in green – all leaping around with an occasional clanging of burning swords and bushel whippings. Atop the hill, the May Queen and Green Man take centre-stage, performing a few ritualistic steps as the gathered oddballs whoop. This all culminates in the Green Man lifting the May Queen into the air and her coronating him with a verdant crown before they light a hoofing great bonfire, initiating the community phase at the Bower, where there's food, booze and merriment.

Edinburgh, Midlothian, Scotland

30 April

Spring

Padstow Obby Oss

A clashing of fiendish fillies at a wild Cornish carnival

If you find yourself stumbling, post-libation, around the bunting-strewn streets of Padstow on 30 April, you may well hear the a cappella strains of the town's 'Night Song' (actually one part of a two-parter called the 'May Song') echoing outside the Golden Lion Inn at midnight. Though merry, its words – 'Unite and unite and let us all unite, for summer is a-come unto day' – herald the imminent unleashing of two errant beasts: the town's Obby Osses.

Come the morning, the two eerie figures of the Red and Blue Ribbon Osses emerge from their stables. Each consists of a circular frame crafted from a wooden hoop almost two metres in diameter, draped in black oilskin, with a tail out back and a grotesque horse's-head mask at the front. The dancer is hidden inside (with only their arms and legs visible), looking out through the mask and wearing a conical hat. The Osses spend the next 12 hours traversing the town, accompanied by ad hoc renditions of the 'Day Song' (which is the second part of the 'May Song'... confusing, I know). To the delight of their respective followers in corresponding blue or red – plus thousands of onlookers – they swoop and flail, led by a Teaser, who jigs in front with a flat paddle as the Osses attempt to 'catch' watching maidens. Every so often, the music will slow and the Oss collapses – though it quickly ratchets up, the Oss leaping back into action ►

May Day festivities and eerie osses (previous) at the Padstow Obby Oss

with yells of 'Oss oss wee oss!' When evening falls, the Osses finally meet at the town's lofty maypole, clashing and then departing back to their stables for a year (and the handler, who must be zapped, presumably retires to bed).

The origins of the OG Red Oss (and the custom in general) are a tad foggy, but there's an oft-repeated story that once, when the chaps of Padstow were out fishing, an ominous French galleon appeared offshore. To scare them off, the women dressed as an Oss, and the wimpy Gauls fled. The Blue Ribbon Oss, meanwhile, was born rather later; devised in the 19th century by a temperance group perturbed by the boozy supporters of his friendly adversary (that is, Red Oss). Regardless of the Osses' hazy beginnings, famous folklorist (and frequent Oss observer) Doc Rowe evocatively described the day as 'a united proclamation – almost a "clenched fist" in the face of time and outside influences'.

Padstow, Cornwall, England
May Day (1 May)

Hastings Jack in the Green

A leaf-covered leviathan welcomes the spring

The verdant behemoth of Jack in the Green first loomed forth in the 1600s. Envious of the flower-covered pails and decorated headdresses sported by rival milkmaids during May Day processions, chimney sweeps began creating ever-larger garlands – the frenzied endpoint of which was a man-sized construction of foliage and flowers, worn by (or perhaps, wearing) a sweep.

The seaside towns of Hastings and St Leonards had two Jack festivals until around 1889, when the tradition fell foul of the Victorians, who were disinclined to the associated drunken hijinks. The custom was revived in 1983 by a Cotswold Morris dancing team – then going by Mad Jack's Morris – and is now stronger than ever. Hundreds stalk the streets in elaborate costumes affixed with animal skulls and plumage, and there are also human maypoles, puppet giants and, of course, Jack himself. With a carved, whiskered visage and a crown of red and white petals, he spins and bounds as his attendants, the foliage-covered 'Bogies', frolic alongside maids in green. Once the parade reaches the crumbling enclaves of Hastings Castle, around 3pm, Jack's leaves are stripped to release the spirit of spring.

Hastings, East Sussex, England
Early May bank holiday weekend

Blackawton International Festival of Worm Charming

Good vibrations in a slippery subterranean contest

'The most fun you can have on your knees in a field,' the organisers wail: we couldn't have put it better. Now in its fourth decade, Blackawton's annual veneration of the squirming soil munchers requires teams of three (the self-explanatory triumvirate of Charmerer, Pickerer and Counterer) to take to a tiny plot of grass and coax its inhabitants to the surface – a modern iteration of the ancient art of 'worm nurdling'. Digging, forking and 'nefarious substances' are banned (the officiating Worm Master can demand charmers taste their own potions), but watering cans, grass-juddering didgeridoos, rakes and bare-fisted pounding are all fair game, so long as the adage of 'Respect the worm!' is followed. The local church bells ring, a worm-centric toast is given at the George Inn and the competition begins: five minutes of 'worming up' followed by a 15-minute charming window. The current record, from 1986, is 149 worms. Impressive, sure, but not a patch on the Guinness World Record of a whopping 567 worms – set by 10-year-old Sophie Smith in 2009, at Cheshire's World Worm Charming Championships.

Blackawton, Devon, England
Sunday of the Early May bank holiday weekend

Oxford University Tortoise Race

Lettuce-chomping contest for the slow and steady

One for the speed freaks. Many Oxford colleges have a beloved pet tortoise, looked after by a student *custos testudinum* (if your Latin's a bit rusty, that's 'tortoise keeper' to you). Campus celebrities, each of them vies for glacially paced stardom in the yearly Tortoise Race, held at Corpus Christi College. The hard-shelled competitors are placed in the middle of a circle made of lettuce leaves and the first to the edge is crowned winner, cheered on by the country's sharpest young minds and future MPs.

This genteel garden party has been a fixture for over 50 years – relatively new compared to Oxford's extant tortoise populace. Tickets are a mere £5 (with proceeds going to charity) and sell out quickly – at a much faster pace than the racing tortoises.

Oxford, Oxfordshire, England
A Sunday in late May or early June

Ely Eel Day

In times past, the city of Ely was technically an island and eel-catching was big business. That mostly went kaput when the surrounding fenlands were drained in the 1800s, but nowadays, a grandiose dedication to its slimy cottage industry lives on with this amusing parade of enormous papier-mâché and textile eels: the world's pre-eminent (and, they say, only) eel day. These anguilliform idols are carried across the green of Ely Cathedral before heading to the town along the banks of the Great Ouse. An eel-flinging contest – mercifully no longer utilising real eels – follows; while various food stalls offer up morsels of the famed fish itself.

Ely, Cambridgeshire, England
Saturday of the Early May bank holiday weekend

Randwick Wap

The Wap (short for wappenshaw, or 'weapon show', as was its original medieval function) is a sweet village fair, revived in the 1970s. Its parade features a cast of local 'celebrities' including a Wap Mayor and Wap Queen – carried through the village en route to a pond dunking – and the infamous Mop-Man, who gleefully flicks water at bystanders with his eponymous tool. The Sunday prior, three Double Gloucester cheeses are blessed at the local church and rolled anticlockwise around the churchyard; one is eaten and the other two are rolled again on the day of the Wap, to predict the fate of the new season's crops.

Randwick, Gloucestershire, England
Second Saturday in May

Helston Flora Day

Pretty formal dances at a floristic shindig

Each year, thousands gather in this Cornish town – its streets, houses and shops all festooned with hazel foliage and bluebells – to gawp at four processional dances, known as 'faddys', performed by locals in their Sunday best.

The festivities commence with the beat of a bass drum at 7am, wherein the first dance, performed by youths in shorts and summer dresses, takes off. There are further dances at 10am, noon and 5pm. The key midday reel, which begins at the Guildhall, is called the Furry Dance. Indeed, the whole hoopla used to be known as Furry Day – 'fer' being Cornish for feast, which tallies, given that this is also St Michael's Day, dedicated to the patron of the parish church.

Aside from the flings, there's also the Hal an Tow, an ancient performance of historical scenes set to archaic songs, staged seven times around town. The most renowned – a generic tale, wrenched into a Helston context – concerns a heavenly fight between St Michael and Satan; the former hoofing a giant rock at the devil, who was knocked down and drowned in the nearby Loe Pool.

Helston, Cornwall, England
8 May (or, if this falls on a Sunday or Monday, the preceding Saturday)

Whitby Penny Hedge

Spindly hedge building with a morbid mythology

The year was 1159. Three hunters were tracking a boar in the Abbot of Whitby's Eskdale Forest, and happened upon a hermitage in the trees. The boar, understandably alarmed, ran in; the hermit slammed the door shut, refusing the men entry. Peeved at being denied their quarry, the hunters beat the hermit – an act of violence he reported to the Abbot before promptly croaking, though not before suggesting the roughs be pardoned if they built a hedge in the town each Ascension Eve, specifically using 'a knife of one penny price' (a simple folding knife).

Fast forward almost nine centuries and Whitby is still at it. Each year, two residents get up at a godawful hour, trudging along the muddy upper harbour near Church Street to fashion an incredibly underwhelming 'hedge' made of hazel and willow. It must be hardy enough to withstand three rising tides and, when it is constructed, a third man blows a horn and yells 'Out on ye!' three times. It's all very prosaic, done with zero theatre, and thus – as esoteric happenings go – even more weirdly entrancing.

Whitby, North Yorkshire, England
Ascension Eve (early May or early June)

Tissington Well Dressing

Petal-flecked decoration of west Derbyshire waterholes

Generally localised to the villages of Derbyshire, well dressing involves the creation of elaborate pictorial scenes on clay-covered boards, which are displayed atop old water wells. Tissington is ground zero, with its six wells decorated in a panoply of imagery. These once mostly depicted biblical narratives but have since branched out, from the bravura exploits of the local mountain rescue team to – checks notes – the Gruffalo and Sonic the Hedgehog.

Irreverent or not, they're arduous to build. Over the course of a week, edged boards are laid out and hammered with hundreds of nails for stability. A layer of clay is kneaded (or 'puddled') into a smooth surface and then covered with sheets of paper, onto which the design is drawn and then pricked in with pins. The outlines are dotted with organic ephemera like seeds, berries or cones, and fleshed out with leaves, petals and mosses, all carefully pressed into the clay bed. The whole icon perishes in situ a week or so later, the clay desiccating and petals withering. Academics surmise that the tradition is possibly pagan or Roman and unbroken for 700 years, but it's hazy as per.

Tissington, Derbyshire, England

Ascension Day, for a week (early May or early June)

He whom this well commemorates was numbered among those who at the call of King and Country
left all
that was dear
to them, endured
hardness, faced
danger, and
finally passed
out of the sight
of men by the
path of duty and
self-sacrifice,
giving up their
own lives that
others might live
in freedom.
Let those who
come after see
to it that his
name be not
forgotten
2017
Coffin
Well

Beating the Bounds

Stone-smacking antics outside the royal stronghold

Back in the medieval and early modern eras, knowing the extent of one's parish bore huge practical and symbolic weight. Each year, communities across the land would traipse around their respective zones to mark their boundaries. Yet the boundary mark between the Tower of London and the parish of All Hallows was historically contested, culminating in a 1698 clash between parishioners.

Nowadays, most are happy to unfold an OS map – but there still exists an urban iteration of the trend around the Tower of London each Ascension Day, where 31 boundary markers are 'beaten'. Following a service in the Tower's chapel, the Chief Yeoman Warder grabs his mace and sets out around the route of the stones, flanked by the Chaplain, an axe-wielding Yeoman Gaoler, two Yeoman Warders, the Governor and some kids with willow wands. At each marker, the words 'Cursed is he who removeth his neighbour's landmark' are followed by the command 'Whack it, boys, whack it!' And whack it they do! Any markers set close to a road are simply pointed at with the mace, and everyone re-enters the Tower at the East Gate to holler the National Anthem on the green and quaff refreshments in the crypt.

Tower of London, London, England
Ascension Day (early May or early June); every three years

High Wycombe Mayor Weigh-In

Ministerial diligence calculated with a giant set of scales

Flagrant body shaming is the name of the game at this municipal take on Weight Watchers, dating back to the 17th century. Heralded by a quarter-peal of the church bells, the Town Crier bellowing and a Sea Cadet merrily drumming away, the inauguration of High Wycombe's new mayor sees them being weighed on a gargantuan set of brass tripod scales. The outgoing incumbent is also weighed: a macebearer announces their original numbers to the crowd, and then shouts 'And some more!' if they've put weight on, or 'And no more!' if they've stayed the same or lost a few pounds (not that it's anybody's business). If they've gained weight, the crowd jeers at the supposed profligacy; if they've lost weight, they applaud, assuming the mayor has been working too hard to take many freebie civil dinners. All the other officials – the town's Charter Trustees and Honorary Burgesses – are popped on the scales, too. This public weigh-in is now held near the Guildhall rather than right outside, as a market has monopolised the space.

High Wycombe, Buckinghamshire, England

Third or fourth Saturday in May

Cooper's Hill Cheese-Rolling

Limb-cracking chase after a wheel of repute

This cheesy event is possibly Britain's most well-known communal custom – certainly the one most beloved of local TV and tabloids (and even Netflix) – for its ankle-shattering potential. An annual rite of passage for lunatic youth, hundreds throw themselves down a vertiginous mount – one of the UK's steepest. All in pursuit of a 3–4 kilogram wheel of Double Gloucester.

It's never actually caught (reaching breakneck speeds of 70–80 miles per hour) but the slapstick capacity for genuinely quite awful injuries is rife. Indeed, the winner of the 2023 ladies' race, one Delaney Irving, was unconscious by the time she reached the bottom, only learning of her victory in the medical tent. There are four downhill races (one for women and three for the more kamikaze men) and three strenuous, cheese-less races back up.

Cheese-rollings were once quite commonplace down big hills and the Cooper's Hill race has been going from the early 1800s or thereabouts. It was banned once, in 1999, for health and safety reasons, but a gang of errant daredevils did it anyway, so it was reinstated the next year.

Brockworth, Gloucestershire, England
Spring bank holiday Monday

Scores of runners partake in the Cooper's Hill Cheese-Rolling event, the victor bagging the rolled wheel of Double Gloucester

Tetbury Woolsack Races

Shaggy sprint up a precipitous hill

Quash any thoughts of the jumping races beloved of kids at school fêtes – Tetbury's big bag contest is rather more exhausting. The town was once a major centre for the Cotswold wool industry; it's said that, back in the 1600s, long-distance herders on their way to Bristol would woo local lasses by knocking back an ale and legging it up Gumstool Hill with a heaving sack of wool (or sometimes a sheep) on their backs. In 1972, the race was incorporated into the Tetbury Festival. Then, it was decreed that the course should run 238 metres from the Royal Oak pub – at the bottom of the steep hill with a whopping 25 per cent gradient – to the Crown, all while carrying a sack of wool, weighing 27 kilograms for the boys and 14 kilograms for the girls. Anyone can enter: the individual races go up once, while relay teams hotfoot it up and down twice. The paucity of entrants (27 men and seven women in 2025) indicates the stamina and thighs required; teams have been fielded by the brawny Pontypool and Stroud rugby clubs, as well as a cohort of Royal Gurkhas.

Tetbury, Gloucestershire, England
Spring bank holiday Monday

BRITISH WOOL
THE SNOOTY FOX

Bampton Morris Dance

Cutting a shine with England's premier folk dance crew

Morris dancing is one of Britain's signature folk pastimes. The sight of ale-soaked old boys camply skipping about, laden with bells and fluttering handkerchiefs, to the lilting wheeze of the melodeon is one of the countryside's more winsome staples. Bampton's Morris crew – relentlessly plying their trade long before the folk dance revival of the early 20th century – have a cast-iron claim to being Britain's definitive troupe. Each Spring bank holiday, six dancers in white jackets with ribboned upper arms and bowler hats, perform one of countless dances (enigmatically called things like 'Lumps of Plum Pudding' and 'Shave the Donkey'). They're watched over by a Fool – who punishes mistakes with a slap on the behind – and a cake bearer, who holds a sword with a whole fruitcake jammed on the end, plus a serrated-edged cake tin to put off anyone tempted by a second wedge. An early account was written up by Rev. J. A. Giles in 1847, who didn't enjoy the spectacle, describing the participants as 'functionaries [who] do nothing but dance and thoroughly fatigue themselves before nightfall'.

Bampton, Oxfordshire, England
Spring bank holiday Monday

The Hunting of the Earl of Rone

An evasive Irish vagabond is returned whence he came

Truly eccentric stuff transpires in this harbourside Devon town each spring since the early 1600s (albeit with a 100-year lull before the 1970s). The titular 'Earl' is probably the Earl of Tyrone, an Irish rogue who fled to Rome and never really had a Devon connection (but who's checking?) Dressed in a horrid mask, with straw-stuffed clothes and a necklace of sea biscuits, he's ritualistically 'hunted' about the town over the weekend by a cohort of grenadier soldiers in tall, ribbon-covered hats and a polka-dot hobbyhorse.

On Monday evening, the Earl is located in Lady's Wood and escorted back to the sea, mounted on a donkey. Along the way, the Grenadiers shoot their guns, and the Earl falls to the ground. The soldiers are elated but the Hobby Horse shows contrition, picking him up and popping him back on. When they eventually reach the beach – after a few beer stops, naturally – he's shot again, but this time his body is hurled into the surf. Morbid, sure, but marvellous fun, with the crowds to prove it.

Combe Martin, Devon, England
Spring bank holiday weekend

Robert Dover's Olimpick Games

A first-rate display of old-school sporting feats

This sweaty smorgasbord of early modern sporting events in Dover's Hill, a beautiful natural amphitheatre, was founded in 1612. Dover was a lawyer who, with the approval of James I, instigated a day of bravura public activities that featured hare-coursing, sledgehammer chucking and, er, chess, among 'em. It's come and gone over the years: nixed by the Puritans, curtailed with enclosure in 1852, reinvigorated in 1966 and active ever since.

These days, events include 'Champion of the Hill' (replete with static jumps and 'Spurning the Barre', a sort of English caber toss), running and tug o' war, all held in the shadow of a stage-style wooden castle. Shin-kicking, a hangover from Dover's days, is the main event: contestants in soft shoes and straw shinpads grab each other by the shoulders and strike at the shins in an attempt to knock the other over. There's some nifty merchandise available and a handy shuttlebus to and from nearby Chipping Campden.

Near Chipping Campden, Gloucestershire, England
First Friday after the Spring bank holiday

Castleton Garland Day

A bell-shaped floral formation is lifted on high

To the High Peaks village of Castleton, where 29 May is Oak Apple Day: a longstanding commemoration of Charles II's restoration to the throne in 1660 (and the kiboshing of all the dour Puritan business that came before). Its denizens have marked the event since the late 1700s with an insane floral parade. A huge bell-shaped construction of flowers and foliage – supposedly in thrall to the oak tree Charles hid in after the Battle of Worcester – is placed over a man (rendered invisible by its size) dubbed the Garland King. He passes through the streets on horseback, accompanied by a Queen in Stuart regalia, some plucky Morris dancers and a silver band. On reaching St Edmund's Church, the garland is pulled up and off with a rope and placed on the tower, with the bush's decorative 'topknot' nipped off and laid to rest in a nearby pub. Punters wishing to realise their floriferous fantasies can apply to be the Garland King, though they must be a parish resident, capable of carrying the gargantuan construct and able to ride a horse 'or willing to learn, at their own expense'.

Castleton, Derbyshire, England
29 May (or, if this falls on a Sunday,
the preceding Saturday or following Monday)

Lancaster
Animal
Feeds

Great Wishford's Oak Apple Day

The uproarious refreshing of ancient foraging rights

In Great Wishford, celebrations of the nationwide Oak Apple Day begin as is tradition here: with a godawful racket. At the break of dawn, a great din is made with pots, pans and shouts around the village – festooned with boughs and bunting – to wake its slumbering populace, who then make for the woods.

This occasion commemorates the historic right of Great Wishford's villagers to collect wood from the former royal forest of Grovely. The bleary-eyed folk dress in period costumes and collect bracken and branches, holding aloft a banner bearing the legend 'Grovely! Grovely! And All Grovely! Unity is Strength'. They then visit Salisbury Cathedral for a ceremonial dance, making claim again to their ancient rights and laying the foraged boughs and twigs on the altar (setting some aside to decorate the church tower and their houses). It's a truly zany throwback to a time when wood was seriously crucial to rural economies (à la Catan). There's also a corresponding village fête, held on the nearest Saturday.

Great Wishford, Wiltshire, England

29 May

GROVELY ! GROVELY ! GROVELY !
AND ALL GROVELY !
UNITY IS STRENGTH

Antient Scorton Silver Arrow

Purportedly the world's longest-held sporting do – with records dating back to 1673 – this is a blokes-only archery tournament (barring a period from 1787 when women were allowed to participate, a privilege which has long since fallen away). The gathered gentleman archers, armed with long, bare and recurve bows, attempt to hit a 3-inch circular black target from 100 yards. The winner is dubbed Captain of the Arrow and is awarded a replica silver arrow (as well as the fun job of organising next year's meet); while the original silver arrow returns home to the Royal Armouries in Leeds until then. Esteemed stuff, but it's terribly genial; competitors mark their own scorecards and can drink, but cursing is strictly forbidden, with the jangling contents of a swear bag donated to charity.

Yorkshire, England (location changes)
A Saturday in mid-to-late May

Maldon Mud Race

By name and by nature, this filthy fun run – first held in 1974 and organised since 2008 by benevolent members of the local Lions and Rotary clubs – sees entrants clad in fancy dress competitively scarpering across half a kilometre of thick River Blackwater gloop during low tide. Anyone can enter – it's £50 a pop to get knee-deep in estuary mulch – but for goodness' sake don't wear your best trousers.

Maldon, Essex, England
April or May, depending on weather and tides

Competitors wade through the mulch at the annual Maldon Mud Race

Summer

Summer's balmy days (well, if we're lucky) lend themselves to much folksy activity. Across the land, gatherings range from the antiquated (such as the benign bowls match in Southampton) to the newfangled (nettle scoffing and scarecrow festivals among them).

Not that it's all fun and games. Summer is also a time of spiritual import – not least at the hallowed sunrise of the solstice – alongside wildlife conservation, rebellion against the ruling classes and truly eerie rituals.

Hawick Common Riding

Cantering tribute to medieval border squabbles

The borderlands between England and Scotland used to be fraught – a hotbed of lawless raiding parties who'd zip across country thresholds to plunder cattle and cause general chaos in a habit called 'reiving'. The rampaging got so tiresome that in Scotland, from the 13th century on, local lairds would appoint someone from their community (or 'burgh') to ride horses around its edges (or 'marches') to stem this encroachment.

These days, the plundering has stopped, but numerous Scottish towns (Coldstream, Dumfries, Jedburgh, Kirkcudbright, Sanquhar, Lanark, Melrose... take your pick) still hold an annual week of commemorative common ridings, celebrating the capture of the English flag at the 1514 Hornshole skirmish, following the Flodden disaster. They've each got their own quirks, not least in the name given to the esteemed 'principal' rider, known variously as the Kelso Laddie in Kelso, the Tub in Newcastleton and the Whipman in West Linton. Hawick's is the first of the year so we'll home in on that one.

The week's events are many, but here's the potted version. In May, the community elects their principal rider, dubbed the Cornet: a young, unmarried man who must remain so for the following three years (when he takes ►

up a secondary job as the Right Hand and then Left Hand Man of the new Cornet).

The common riding week proper, though, is at the beginning of June. Its schedule is dense, but the collected rituals include: a few cantering 'chases' across hill and field; the integral 'colour bussing', where ribbons are tied to the Cornet's staff by his 'lass' and some maids of honour; proclamations of his duties from the town hall balcony; the distribution of snuff from a big horn mull (an old Scottish tobacco container made from a ram's horn); the elaborately dressed Cornet and his followers piling into the purpose-built St Leonard's Hut for the traditional refreshments of 'curds and cream'; the cutting of sod (a slab of turf) to mark the burgh's borders; and, of course, heaps of ceremonial horse riding and ribbon-clad flag-waving (especially on the important final days). That's scratching the surface, really – but safe to say, it's an undertaking of startling local pride and brilliant dedication.

Scottish Borders and southern counties, Scotland
Early June (but with preamble in May)

Mayor of Ock Street

Anti-authoritarian elections and a whole lotta Morris

The 'mock mayor' was a historic election ritual, where communities would vote in their own informal 'officials' to goad the municipal haughtiness of the real thing. They were largely tanked by the 1835 Municipal Reform Act, but an election at Ock Street – once a rundown part of Abingdon – continues.

Only the district's residents and members of Abingdon's Traditional Morris Dancers group can vote, and the winner is always a Morris man (and for much of its history, a member of the Hemmings family, a local lineage who have kept the tradition alive). A polling station is set up at the group's Brewery Tap HQ and voting happens between 10am and 4pm; the crosses are quickly counted and the new mayor is carried up and down the street in a flower-covered chair. There's plenty of jaunty Morris dancing from guest teams and the Abingdon men themselves, who carry the Horns of Ock Street – the iconic byproduct of a 1700 grudge, wherein two local groups fought over the head and horns of a roasted ox, with the Ock Street lads prevailing. The horns are mounted on a wooden bovine head and brought out specially to be danced with on the day.

Abingdon, Oxfordshire, England
Closest Saturday to the summer solstice (21 June)

1700

Appleby Horse Fair

Europe's largest gathering of Romany and Travellers is a week-long equine exposition without parallel. Originating in an 18th-century livestock market called the New Fair, there's trading of all kinds – from harnesses to actual horses – plus the drawing of ornate vardo wagons, traditional music and fortune-telling. Attendees are invariably drawn to Long Marton Road (aka the 'flashing lane', where horses are paraded) and the Sands, a spot on the River Eden where the steeds are washed. Make sure to visit on the Friday, Saturday or Sunday, when all the action happens.

Appleby-in-Westmorland, Cumbria, England
Early June, from Thursday to the following Wednesday

Glastonbury Festival

The sheer scope and cultural fervour around Britain's definitive music festival – as anyone who's sat online with ten browsers open in the futile pursuit of tickets can attest – warrant its 'modern folk gathering' status. But hedonism aside, a spiritual aspect remains – not least at the Healing Field. An 'elemental mandala', the field is split into Air, Water, Earth and Fire areas, replete with holistic workshops, healing arts (including shiatsu, craniosacral massage and reiki), medical herbalism, shamanic journeying and cacao ceremonies, as well as Soothsayers' Avenue (a destination for Tarot, Angel, Palm and Rune readings).

Pilton, Somerset, England
Late June

Spiritual connection at the Healing Field, Glastonbury Festival

Summer Solstice

See in the sunrise over antiquarian stones

The summer solstice marks the arrival of the year's longest day and shortest night – a transitional lynchpin, after which the evening light fades incrementally earlier and the inexorable road back to winter begins. Due to the sun's integral role in crop cycles, it was a time of huge importance to our agrarian ancestors; it's believed that many Neolithic and Bronze Age stone circles and tombs were built in architectural accordance with the position of the day's sunrise.

It remains an event of spiritual and countercultural significance – and Stonehenge is, of course, the big one. As much festival as polytheistic observance, it attracts a real cross-section of the populace – from druids and 'allotment biker' types to ravers, children, neo-antiquarians and yawning tourists – all gathered to see the sun peek over the top of the complex's 'heel stone', just outside of the main circle, at around 4:45am. It's incredibly well organised – there's ample parking (albeit with a schlep through the rolling greenery of this sacred, mound-dotted landscape), coffee stalls and even a merchandise tent.

Other revellers make for nearby Avebury, where a leviathan assortment of stone rings, geometric avenues and earthworks run through the village. Sunrise here is a bit less hectic and more family orientated, encouraging greater exploration of the sprawling site, with the Kings Drummers pounding in the sunset before the 21st proper. ▶

Solstice celebrations at Stonehenge, with revellers basking in the early morning sun

Over in Wales, the solstice is known as Heuldro'r Haf. Anglesey's astounding Bryn Celli Ddu ('Mound of the Dark Grove') – a monumental Neolithic burial chamber – is a sensational place to see it. Once a year, on the solstice, early rays shine down the tomb's narrow passage for about 20 minutes, illuminating the chamber inside. Meanwhile, the Anglesey Druid Order light a bowl of fire in emulation of the sun and make offerings to the realms of sea, sky and land.

Those festivities aside, there's a real notion of making your own adventure for the solstice – simply drag yourself early doors to any ancient monument and feel the connection to the cosmic turn of the seasons. The winter solstice, on 21 December, also sees similar – though much smaller and chillier – communal events at the same locales.

Various locations

21 June

World Nettle Eating Championship

Scrumptious stingers in the West Dorset wilds

Riotously immortalised in Hugh Fearnley-Whittingstall's surprisingly affecting back-to-the-land jaunt *Return to River Cottage* in 2000, the Bottle Inn's annual nettle eating contest remains a mouth-stinging, beer-sloshing mainstay for the brave folk of this West Dorset village. The rules are painfully simple (or simply painful). Contestants must pull the leaves from two-foot-long nettle stems, munching them and washing them down with as much tepid ale as necessary (people have also reportedly blasted their taste buds with chilli sauce prior, for a sneaky advantage and it's said that the nettles can turn one's mouth black). Whoever has the greatest cumulative length of bare nettle stems after an hour is the winner; the 2025 women's victor, first-timer Lucy Dermody, set a Guinness World Record, stripping 68 feet of the stuff. The contest was first held in 1986 – supposedly arising from an argument between two farmers over whose nettles were longest, with one of them swearing to devour any stinger longer than his own.

Marshwood, Dorset, England

Late June

No 1
NETTLE
EATING
ROOKIE

Whalton Baal Fire

Bonfire dancing and a spooky straw icon

Whalton marks Old Midsummer's Eve on 4 July – a legacy of Britain adopting the Gregorian calendar in 1752 – with a whacking great bonfire, traditionally celebrating the successful gathering of the corn harvest. School children would dance around the bonfire, and young couples would leap over it for its supposed fertility-bolstering properties. More paganistic still, until World War I, they'd also throw an unsettling corn effigy called a Kern Baby – a humanoid figure with a 'head' of wheat sheaves, wrapped in a fine, billowing white dress – into the inferno to appease the gods.

These days, the leaping is gone but the bonfire and dancing remain; apparently it's the only localised midsummer blaze of its kind to still be active since 1903. The Kern Baby tradition was inadvertently revived by artist Faye Claridge. Inspired by haunting Victorian photographs of the original Baby, Claridge created a resplendent 15-foot-tall version, brought home to Whalton in 2016 to mark the Queen's 90th birthday (lucky her). The village has fashioned one each July since, albeit in a more decorative form, and popped it outside the communal hall instead of being reduced to cinders.

Whalton, Northumberland, England
4 July

Sma' Shot Day

A shawl weaver's holiday in a famous mill town

Back in the mid-1800s, Paisley was a hotbed for the weaving trade. An integral part of the shawl-making process was sewing in 'sma' shot', a fine yarn paid for by the weavers, without compensation. Up in arms, they demanded retribution, which they received on 1 July 1856 when a new table of prices was published. Traditionally, the weavers and their families would take a Saturday in July off, ambling to the local station with marching bands and banners en route to the seaside ('doon the watter' in local parlance). After the sma' shot triumph, this holiday – solidified as the first Saturday in July – became known as Sma' Shot Day and continued even as the shawl-weaving trade diminished.

The merciful introduction of the five-day week in the 1930s killed it off a bit, but the custom was revived in 1986 and is now marked with a vivid annual parade. Eye-poppingly huge weaver puppets are led through town to the cavernous bashing of a giant single drum, and a top-hatted and red-jacketed effigy (called the 'Cork') – representing the weavers' domineering industrial bosses – is burned on the town green.

Paisley, Renfrewshire, Scotland
First Saturday in July

Grasmere Rushbearing

A floral tribute to years of fetid church flooring

Historically, before the luxury of flagstones, church floors were made of dirt – filthy, hugely uncomfortable for the congregations (as pews hadn't been invented yet either) and occasionally stinking, not least since the dead were often interred beneath them. To counter this, churchwardens would be tasked with periodically laying down rushes (a kind of long, grassy wetland plant), replacing them on important days. The introduction of proper paving curtailed the calling, but it lives on symbolically in some parishes – particularly in Grasmere, the epicentre of contemporary rushbearing.

In honour of St Oswald, the parish church's patron saint, a cheery parade of locals makes its way to the church, holding aloft images of him in floral frames, Latin proclamations on woven banners and bundles of rushes and 'bearings' shaped like hearts, harps and maypoles. The rushes are laid on the altar and affixed to the pews and the 'Hymn for the Rush Bearers' is sung. At the centre of it all are the Rush Maidens – six young lasses in woody-green dresses and flower-dotted straw hats, carrying a white sheet laden with the rushes – who are rewarded for their efforts with some famous Grasmere gingerbread.

Grasmere, Cumbria, England
Second Saturday in July

World Peashooting Championship

Pucker up for this pea-blowing bonanza

For over 50 years, this annual contest has brought hap-pea-ness to participants and spectators alike. It was inaugurated in 1971 by school headmaster John Tyson, who, after catching his pupils firing peas at one another with straws, decided to put their sharpshooting skills to better use, founding a yearly peashooting championship at the village fête.

Now, it's an internationally renowned event. The basic guidelines are that peashooters mustn't exceed 12 inches in length, and only peas bought at the contest can be fired (for £1 a bag). Be warned: all peas can – and from round three on, *will* – be spot checked. Participants blow through the peashooter at a round target 3.7 metres away; the inner ring scores five points, the middle three and the outer one.

Nuance creeps in with the two key rounds: the Traditional and the Open (other rounds include the adorably named Petit Pois for primary schoolers). The Traditional dictates plain peashooter tubes, while the Open allows for customised shooters in the hope of gaining an advantage. Low-grade lasers are fine, as are balance aids and handles, and past events have seen a panoply of add-ons, including brick-sized monstrosities covered in Lego.

Witcham, Cambridgeshire, England
Second Saturday in July

Riders

Swan Upping

Cygnet weighing on the glistening Thames

Killing swans is a famously treasonous and diabolical act – and apart from the British Crown, three other bodies technically have ownership over the wondrous waterfowl. Two of these – the City of London's distinguished Worshipful Companies of Vintners and Dyers – set off up the Thames with the King's Swan Marker each summer for the esteemed tradition of Swan Upping.

Over five days, the collective Swan Uppers travel 79 miles from Sunbury to Abingdon (past idyllic spots like Goring, Marlow and Henley) in wooden rowing skiffs, laboriously rounding up the river's dinky communities of mute swans and cygnets to assess their health, check for injuries and mark them for respective ownership by the Crown and the two livery companies.

It's all charmingly ceremonial. The King's Swan Marker dresses in full nautical regalia, with his men in red and their boats flying a majestic white flag with the royal cypher. The Vintners wear white and are overseen by their own Swan Marker, and the Dyers are decked out in Breton-style white and blue stripes and commanded by their Barge Master. Both groups fly fine, swan-emblazoned company pennants. (The actual rowers, meanwhile, are members of the river's Company of Watermen and Lightermen, but they don't own any swans.)

When a family of swans is found, the Uppers all yell 'All up!' and gently surround them with their boats, ►

before carrying them ashore for their examinations – swans, you see, are susceptible to all kinds of hazards, from errant fishing tackles to oil slicks and dog attacks. The downy cygnets are weighed in little textile hammocks and, after the King's Swan Warden establishes who owns which set of parents, he divvies up the brood accordingly. The livery company reps place their own rings around the cygnets' feet, while any left unmarked belong to HRH.

The whole sun-dappled hoo-hah began way back in the 12th century – cygnets were then prized for their bijou eating qualities – with the two livery companies gaining ownership rights in the late 1400s. While mating pairs have dwindled since the mid-20th century, it remains a heartwarming conservation effort, attended by scores of local school children and, occasionally, the reigning monarch. It's almost enough to bring a patriotic tear to one's eye (almost).

Sunbury, Surrey to Abingdon, Oxfordshire, England
Third week in July

Moulton Crow Fair

Cavorting corvids and a sentient scarecrow

Kooky avian action takes centre stage at this sunny jamboree, in which a troupe of 16 villagers – the 'crows' themselves, dressed entirely in black, with beaks sewn onto their masks – perform a choreographed circular dance around a living 'scarecrow'. A (real) farmer enters the scene and is met with some unnerving avian shrieking, before shooting one of the crows dead (not real). The rest flutter around a bit longer, then everyone saunters off, the scarecrow included.

It all began in the 1920s, devised by some laid-off salt workers as a peculiar means of drumming up a bit of cash around Cheshire's country fairs. The sentient scarecrow was a 1929 addition to the crow dance, which was then dubbed The Relics of the Corn Field. A few years later, the name changed to Moulton Young Rooks and, after World War II, the Moulton Crows. The dancers are all technically anonymous but it's an esteemed role and 'people who were once crows as kids will not hesitate to tell you', as was explained by Crow No. 6 in a 2024 interview with the *Northwich Guardian*.

Moulton, Cheshire, England
Second Saturday in July

Berwick Curfew Run

Long ago, evening curfew bells would ring out in towns and villages across the land, with locals rushing home to dampen their hearths and get to bed before the next interminable day of toil. Up in Berwick, it still rings every day at 8pm (and has done since the time of William the Conqueror). In the 1990s, a local running group devised this short annual race: an eminently manageable 1.28 miles around the town's Elizabethan walls, to be completed within the bell's 13-minute pealing.

Berwick, Northumberland, England
A Wednesday in early July

St Wilfrid's Feast Procession

One of the country's oldest annual gatherings (they reckon) dates way back to 1108, when Henry I granted a charter to the city of Ripon for a grand feast celebrating its patron saint, St Wilfrid – whether it was to mark his birthday or his return from exile in 705 CE is up for discussion. Nowadays, it's a heaving carnival, featuring decorated lorries, dancers and marching bands, attracting a whopping 50,000 people in busy years.

Ripon, North Yorkshire, England
Last Saturday in July or first Saturday in August

Bread Ahead Lammas Day

Rise and shine at Borough Market's best bakery

Lammas (or 'loaf mass' in Old English) is an old-school Christian gathering that acknowledges the year's first wheat harvest. Some folk who really do know their edible grains are the artisan bakers of London's Bread Ahead, in Borough Market. Each year, they pay their dues with a delectable bread-based ceremony. First, the Dean of Southwark Cathedral zips across the marketplace to bless the bakery, its staff, its associated millers and farmers (Marriage's, near Chelmsford, which does both), and some newly delivered wheat grain, which he then assists in milling into flour to make a Lammas Day 'Cathedral Loaf'. When this is risen and cooked, everyone tootles off to the church itself for a thanksgiving service, with the loaf and a wheatsheaf in tow, the irresistible fragrance of freshly baked carbs wafting as they go.

It's a rather lovely meeting of antiquated and modern, not least as Bread Ahead is one of the hipper bakeries in this part of town. Some would suggest that their hallowed doughnuts are an even greater offering to the gods.

Southwark, London, England

1 August

National Eisteddfod of Wales

A druidic convention in celebration of Welsh culture

'The Welsh,' declared Evelyn Waugh in *Decline and Fall*, his rip-roaring comedic novel of 1928, 'are the only nation in the world that has produced no graphic or plastic art, no architecture, no drama. They just sing.' Mean! But also untrue, as the enormous annual outdoor National Eisteddfod proves. Founded in 1861, it's Europe's biggest cultural gathering: a sprawling celebration of Welsh-language poetry, dancing, essays, literature and spoken word that, according to the National Museum of Wales, can be traced back to a bardic competition held by Lord Rhys of Cardigan Castle in 1176.

These days, it happens at a different location in Wales each year and attracts around 170,000 attendees. The elaborate main events are organised by the Gorsedd of the Bards, a druidic cultural society founded in 1792 in, er, London's Primrose Hill by Welsh academic Iolo Morganwg, as a means of preserving the country's ancient Celtic heritage. Members include national icons such as opera singer Bryn Terfel, Paralympian Tanni Grey-Thompson and rugby beefcake George North.

In a purpose-made ring of 12 facsimile 'stones' with a central altar stone called the Maen Llog, the Archdruid (head of the Gorsedd) presides over three key ceremonies: the Crowning (presented for a poem of up to 250 lines, in a freestyle metre known as *pryddest*); the Prose Medal (normally for a novel or short-story collection); and the Chairing of the Bard (for the finest *awdl*, a long-form poem in a traditional Welsh poetic metre termed *cynghanedd*). The winners are plonked into resplendently carved thrones – with new meticulous crowns, medals and chairs designed by artisans each year – and the victorious literati honked in with the *Corn Gwlad* (a merry cacophony of long trumpets) and treated to a floral dance by some local kiddies.

Elsewhere, there are more hyper-druidic hijinks like the *Corn Hirlas* – a wine-filled horn of plenty presented to the Archdruid to welcome the Gorsedd to the Eisteddfod – and the reveal of a huge Grand Sword, only partly unsheathed as a symbol of peace. The archaic pageantry, everyone clad in their druidic robes, is wild – and the whole esoteric caboodle one in the eye for those cynics who still consider Shirley Bassey to be Wales's greatest cultural export.

Wales (location changes)

First week in August

Mary Gibson's Mausoleum Inspection

Bizarre bequests at a south London graveyard

In her will of 7 December 1786, Mary Gibson left a then sizeable £500 to the church of St Nicholas, on the proviso that each year the local vicar would do a special sermon before ritualistically checking the condition of the now Grade-II listed mausoleum hosting her and her family, repairing it if necessary. And so it remains today: every year, a small cohort still traipses through the churchyard, opening the mausoleum (a rather bare room with a few dusty coffins, which some say is haunted by a giant toad) with a key presented on a red cushion by a choirboy. From 1985, there was a 20-year fallow period – the incumbent vicar deeming the whole thing undignified and doing the checks solo, and his even grumpier successor banning it outright on account of the paganistic and 'queer' vibe – but a host of Gibson stans saw it reinstated, and it's now going strong again.

Sutton, London, England

12 August

Burning of Bartle

A fiery end for an apocryphal scoundrel

Pity Old Bartle! Every year, following a sweaty fell race and daytime gala, his doomed effigy – dowdy straw-filled clothes, with a white mask and desperate eyes – is paraded around this North Yorkshire village. He is then led up a little road, where he's stabbed, doused in petrol and burned – all while a local decked up as a Green Man merrily toots on some pipes. Quite what Bartle did to deserve it is unclear: some say he represents a centuries-old cattle rustler or swine thief caught in the stony scar of Penhill Crags. Others think he was a giant or St Bartholomew himself, which seems unlikely, given the 'real' Bart was one of Jesus's disciples. Whatever, it's been happening for around 400 years, with hundreds of visitors gathering annually to form the seething mob. The story of his horrid demise is described in lurid verse, read out at the parade's various pub stops:

On Penhill Crags he tore his rags / At Hunters Thorn he blew his horn / At Capplebank Stee he brock his knee / At Grisgill Beck he brock his neck / At Wadham's End he couldn't fend, at Grisgill End we'll mek his end! / Shout lads Shout!

Grisly, eh?

West Witton, North Yorkshire, England
A Saturday close to St Bartholomew's Day (24 August)

The Burryman Procession

A burr-covered brute parades on the banks of the Forth

Few sights in the folk calendar are as unnerving as the Burryman: a stout Scottish gent covered entirely, but for his boots, in a dense carpet of sticky burdock seeds (plus assorted bits of foliage, ferns and holly berries).

Every year for four centuries, this otherworldly icon has been led around South Queensferry, on the southern bank of the Firth of Forth bay, the day before the town's eponymous fair. Come fair day, he travels seven miles in nine hours, starting at the Stag Head Hotel and ending at the Forth Bridge, calling at houses and hostelries as he goes.

He's accompanied by two handlers in kilts, who hold onto his flower-laden staffs (so that he may keep his arms aloft) – a knackering Christ-like pose that prevents the burrs from falling off. A bell ringer soundtracks his journey, and excitable locals yell 'Hip, hip, hooray! It's the Burryman's day!' as he approaches and offer him drams of whisky (through a straw) and coins.

It's wackadoodle stuff, though the symbology is vague: some surmise he's a Green Man-like fertility symbol, a means to ward off evil spirits, or perhaps a sacrificial victim of some kind.

South Queensferry, Edinburgh, Scotland

Second Friday in August

STEWART CLARK AVENUE

Kettlewell Scarecrow Festival

A haystack's worth of scarecrows in the Yorkshire Dales

Likely inspiration for the classic first episode of rural mockumentary *This Country* (to BBC iPlayer, quick!), this North Yorkshire village plays host to hundreds of scarecrows in its annual festival. The spectacle attracts thousands of visitors, who can track down the scarecrows along two mapped trails.

The festival was inaugurated in 1994 as a fundraiser for the local primary school; each year brought more scarecrows, and ever more elaborate creations. From an electrician with a fizzing fuse-box (fire hazard or what) and a scene from *Call the Midwife* to a doomed Jack and Rose on the stern of the Titanic, Kettlewell's seen it all.

Kettlewell, North Yorkshire, England
A week in mid-August

Cilgerran Coracle Races

A coracle is a small, lightweight, single-occupant boat with a basketwork frame, roped together and covered in bitumen-slathered hide or canvas – a bit like an upturned turtle shell. They're heavily associated with Wales, a heritage marked each year with a feverish coracle race down the River Teifi – dating back to 1950 – as part of Cilgerran Festive Week. A 1961 video of the event, on the BFI website, is especially vibey: a vision of retro bob hairdos and children weeping over dropped ice creams, all watching racers drag their oars through the water's placid levels.

Cilgerran, Pembrokeshire, Wales
Penultimate or final Saturday in August

St Bartholomew's Bun Race

Late each August, the children of Sandwich partake in a jovial outdoor footrace around the town's historic almshouse. They're each given a currant bun by the mayor for their trouble, while adults receive a hard biscuit decorated with the town's coat of arms. It all harks back to a sea battle of 1217 in which the Brits trounced the French, the winnings of which were spent on building said almshouse. A 'pricking in' with a silver bodkin of a new master (that is, a nominal caretaker), chosen from its 16 residents, still happens before the low-key athletics.

Sandwich, Kent, England
24 August (or, if this falls at the weekend, the preceding Friday or following Monday)

Knighthood of the Old Green

A cheery bowls match on the world's oldest pitch

Possibly the only interesting thing to regularly happen in Southampton, this archaic bowls match has been played since the 1700s on the city's Old Green, allegedly the world's oldest bowling turf. The rules slightly deviate from the norm. A flattened jack is placed on a penny and each player (called 'Gentleman Commoners') bowls two balls (or 'woods') at it, with the distance to the jack measured on each turn. If someone hits the jack, it's simply popped back on the penny. After everyone has bowled, the winner of that 'end' is declared; the jack is then moved, and everyone bowls at it from its previous position. The first player to win seven 'ends', which can take days, is declared the victor and becomes a Knight of the Old Green – and subsequently banned from playing again, though they are obliged to organise and judge the following year's tourney (in morning dress, with a black top hat, no less). The city mayor, town crier and other official types mill around while the game's on. Visitors are welcome, and it always happens on a Wednesday.

Southampton, Hampshire, England

A Wednesday in late August

Kilwinning Papingo Shoot

Vertical sharpshooting at an unfortunate pigeon target

Every year, the estimable Ancient Society of Kilwinning Archers – founded back in 1483 – partakes in a vertiginous competition at the ruins of Kilwinning's medieval Abbey. The Papingo is a wooden pigeon, placed on a perch sticking out from the top of the 35-metre-tall abbey tower. Directly below, archers with low-powered long bows and blunt arrows (wearing red-bobbled tam o' shanter hats) place a foot on the stone doorway steps and fire upwards at the wretched bird.

The first archer to smack it off the perch – or 'ding doun the doo' – within a two-hour timeframe is the winner, declared Captain of the Papingo and gifted the ornate Walker Trophy, a brilliantly sculpted model of the tower (prior to this, the prize was a different trophy, replete with a silver arrow dating from 1724, and dangling with nearly 200 previous winners' medals). Then, the bird is re-mounted; and second and third place awarded to whoever can shoot off each of its removable wings, each receiving a dashing rosette for their skills.

Kilwinning, Ayrshire, Scotland
A weekend in June or August

Aberaeron Mackerel Fiesta

A fishy funeral on the mid-Wales coastline

The storied fishing traditions of this tract of Welsh coastline stretch back to the monks of Strata Florida, a nearby Cistercian abbey founded in 1164, whose old fish traps can still be seen at low tide near the village of Aberaeron. The waters here remain rich in mackerel, and the silvery shoals are given a grand end-of-season 'funeral' each August.

As the sun dips, the Cardiff Adamant Jazz Band strikes up a tune and trundles the streets, accompanying the procession of a 7-metre-long papier-mâché mackerel – carried by six 'pallbearers' in harlequin masks and pork pie hats (the mackerel has one, too), and followed by a group of wailing 'widows' representing the fishermen's wives left ashore. When it reaches the yacht club, the vicar gives a speech about mackerel (and the necessity of sea life conservation in general), at which point the colossal fish is laid down on the beach and set alight, returning it to the sea whence it came.

Aberaeron, Ceredigion, Wales
Summer bank holiday weekend

HARBOURMASTER HOTEL

Birnam World Haggis-Eating Championship

This one's self-explanatory: a gluttonous game of offal-gorging and a highlight of Birnam's longstanding Highland Games, held since 1864. Anyone can enter, and whoever scarfs the gutsy pudding quickest wins. If any haggis drops on the floor or table, you're out; and once it's devoured, the victor must keep it all down for 30 seconds. Everyone guzzles lubricating lager as they go, all the while being volubly taunted by the MC for their techniques.

Birnam, Perth and Kinross, Scotland
Last Saturday in August

World Bog Snorkelling Championships

Forty years in, the globe's murkiest swimming race – held in the Waen Rhydd peat bog – attracts competitors from as far afield as South Africa, Serbia and Australia. The costumes are varied – from toilet bowls to Barbie dolls – but the objective is simple: doggy-paddle there and back across a muddy trench (120 yards total) as swiftly as possible. Rules abound – one's head, for example, must remain underwater except for the occasional 'look' – and if it's a tie, there's a final 'bog-off'. The Guinness World Record was set in 2023 by Neil Rutter: a speedy 1 minute and 12.35 seconds.

Near Llanwrtyd Wells, Powys, Wales
Summer bank holiday weekend

A swimmer participates in a doggy-paddle race across a Welsh peat bog

Bramble Bank Cricket Match

Sopping wet wickets in the middle of the sea

For over 40 years, Hamble-le-Rice's Royal Southern Yacht Club and the Isle of Wight's Island Sailing Club have met for a jolly summer game of cricket – the kooky USP being its setting on Bramble Bank: a pointy, 200-metre-long sandbar in the middle of the Solent.

It all happens at the lowest spring tide – normally in August – when the sandbar appears from the depths for an hour or so, at which point the players and spectators head off in a flotilla to their makeshift pitch and drenched outfield. They knock out as many runs as possible, only downing tools again when the water rises and the field gets a bit splashy – grabbing their wickets, balls, dogs, children and booze, and motoring back to their respective clubhouses.

The first match was organised in the 1950s by dinghy-sailing pioneer Uffa Fox; and, given how unsuited the setting is to any serious sporting endeavour, the teams merely take it in turns to be the pre-designated 'winner'.

Between Cowes on the Isle of Wight and Southampton Water
in the middle of the Solent, England
Late August or early September, depending on tides

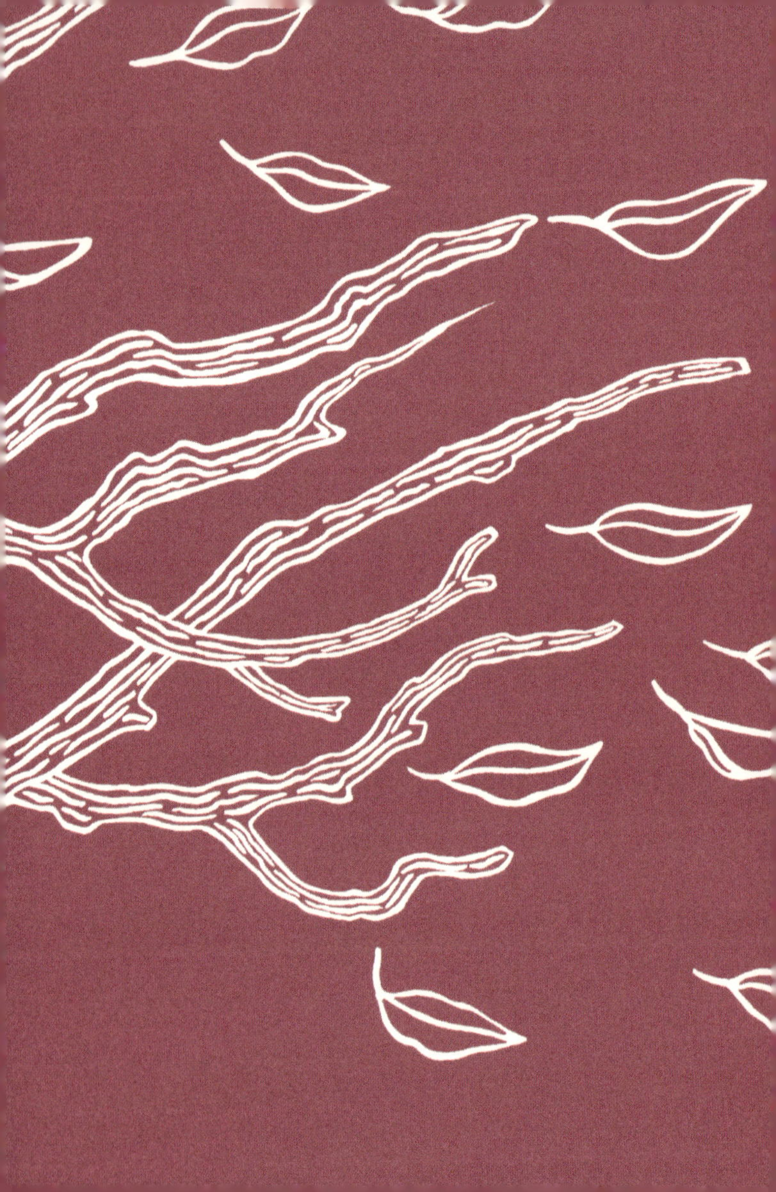

Autumn

The autumn equinox – when day and night are equal in length – is a significant agrarian and spiritual event for pagan and druidic communities across Britain. Many folk rituals at this time of year mark the end of the harvest – a jovial period of feasting and expressing gratitude to nature. At the close of October arrive Samhain (the ancient Celtic segue to winter) and Halloween (or All Hallows' Eve), followed by the more modern but equally widespread Guy Fawkes Night, or Bonfire Night.

Crying the Neck

A pagan prayer to the harvest in rural Cornwall

For centuries, communities across Cornwall marked the completion of the year's harvest with an arcane ritual called Crying the Neck – a highlight of the ancient agricultural festival of Guldize. Crying declined with the mechanisation of farming, but the practice was revived by various Cornish heritage groups in the 1920s.

These days – in places like Zennor, Madron and Helston – a prayer to the year's harvest is read in Cornish and English by the vicar, followed by a contextual reading on the ritual's latent pagan sentiments. The last sheaves of corn are scythed from the ground. Bundled and held aloft, the golden handful is presented to the four points of the compass: to the north (representing winter), east (for the sowing of springtime crops), south (the highest point of the sun) and west (for the harvest). At each, a chant of 'I 'ave 'un! / What 'ave 'ee? / A neck!' is hollered three times by a master of ceremonies and the gathered folk. Then, there's tea, or – if sticking with convention – gallons of local 'zider'.

Across Cornwall, England
Late August to mid-September

Throwing the Feat Stone

Rugged rock tossing at a dinky Denbighshire church

'Stone lifting' has long been a fad in North Wales: the heaving of unwieldy boulders in trials of dexterity and brute strength is a historic rite of passage in the transition from youth to manhood. This brawny custom, known as Y Maen Camp, or 'Feat Stone', lives on at the compact chapel of St Michael and All Angels in the Vale of Clwyd.

It's rather straightforward: each autumn around *Gwyl-mabsant* (the village's saint day), a rounded 45-kilogram stone is dragged from its resting place by the altar to the north side of the churchyard, where fewer headstones risk being smashed. Instruments are sounded to 'wake the saint' and a strapping contender then lifts the stone and attempts to chuck it as far as possible backwards over their head. The victor becomes the 'parish champion', to polite applause from the local audience.

Other notable examples of barely liftable stones include Garreg Orchest, kept in an Anglesey pub called Y Goron (you're obliged to buy a pint after lifting it), and the egg-shaped Criccieth Stone, which weighs a back-breaking 177.5 kilograms.

Efenechtyd, Denbighshire, Wales

A weekend in late September or early October

Braemar Highland Gathering

Hefty heavies and caber-chucking in the Highlands

Hoots! Nothing evokes the spirit of the glen like a Highland games – and Braemar's are the definitive staging. Rugged gatherings have happened here for almost 1,000 years, but the present form was established in 1832 and has been regularly attended by the reigning British monarch – acclaimed as the 'Chieftain of the Gathering' – since 1848.

Historic illustrations of the games from the 1830s depicted a traditional bash in the shadow of Braemar Castle, awash with kilts, sporrans (a traditional pouch attached to a kilt) and bobbled tam o' shanter hats. Not much has changed. Spectators can expect the full gamut of jolly Gaelic pastimes: reedy piping by men in huge furry bonnets; the foot-loose flurry of Highland dancers; monolithically muscle-bound and kilted 'heavies' chucking cabers, throwing hammers and putting the heaving Braemar Stone; hill running, tugs of war and other more conventional athletics. And all in a beatific northern setting within the rolling foothills of the Cairngorms, to boot. Both standing and seated tickets – the latter with ringside views and, crucially, rain coverage – are available from the Gathering's official website.

Braemar, Aberdeenshire, Scotland
First Saturday in September

Colne Oyster Fisheries Opening Ceremony

Oysters have been a prized spoil of Essex's estuaries since Roman times – not least in the tidal inlets of Mersea Island and the River Colne, home of Colchester's oyster fishery. Each year since 1540, the season has been opened by the town's mayor drifting out in a boat to pull up the first prized bivalves, before reading an ancient charter (granted to the town by Richard I in 1189 to regulate the industry) and wolfing a load of gingerbread and gin.

Colchester, Essex, England
First Friday in September

World Stone Skimming Championships

A former quarry on the teeny Inner Hebridean island of Easdale has played host to the annual World Stone Skimming Championships since 1983 – drawing participants from as far afield as the US, Sri Lanka and Zimbabwe. Rules insist that the stones be made of Easdale slate, sea-worn and 3 inches maximum in diameter (measured with a metal 'ring of truth'). The event was 'rocked' in 2025 by a tampering scandal, some stones having been shaped into 'suspiciously circular' forms...

Easdale Island, Firth of Lorn, Scotland
Early September

Skimming stones and dodging scandals at the World Stone Skimming Championships

Sowerby Bridge Rushbearing

A resplendent rushcart does the Calder Valley rounds

As in Grasmere (p.98), the symbolic tradition of rushbearing continues heartily in the town of Sowerby Bridge. The USP here is the monumental rushcart itself. Fashioned to a 1906 design (the year the tradition was revived), it's a steampunk/pagan mashup on two wheels, densely thatched and towering 16 feet high. The cart is ridden by a bevy of local gals and pulled by 60 men in Panama hats and clogs, with a range of ropes and poles to stop it rolling calamitously downhill. They're followed by a gang of cheer-ons in Edwardian dress, soundtracked by lilting accordions and bells, with intermittent distractions in the form of mummers, Morrisers and sword dancers.

The procession takes around 14 hours, starting with a blessing at the neighbouring village of Warley on Saturday, before heading to Sowerby Bridge. On Sunday morning, a bundle of rushes is presented in the church, and the cart heads over the tops to Cotton Stones, Triangle and Ripponden – culminating at the Old Bridge Inn for a well-deserved pint (or four). For visitors, the timing, route and particular entertainments are listed on the Sowerby Rushbearing website before the event each year.

Calder Valley, West Yorkshire, England

First weekend in September

Marldon Apple Pie Fair

Pomaceous princesses and a grand dedicatory dessert

Founded in the 1800s, revived in 1958 and a yearly mainstay ever since, Marldon Apple Pie Fair is a winsome village fête with a fruity quirk. Back in the 19th century, local apple-man George Hill – known for transporting panniers full of his blushing bounty to nearby Torquay by way of donkey – began donating a gargantuan apple pie to the fair each year. The prodigious pudding – carried in a flower-festooned cart drawn by two black donkeys with decorated reins – was cut by an Apple Pie Princess, marking the opening of the fête.

The pie has changed form over the years: in 1935, the *Transactions of the Devonshire Association* described it as oval-shaped and the size of a kitchen table, while at subsequent fairs it consisted of hundreds of individual pies. Today, it's rectangular, arriving via a charming red-and-custard cart pulled by local primary schoolers whenever the donkeys are AWOL. The Princess follows in tow, clad in a matching claret cloak and dinky tiara. After the big reveal, the pie is sliced up and sold with dollops of regionally de rigueur clotted cream.

Marldon, Devon, England
First Saturday in September

Abbots Bromley Horn Dance

Eerie-arcane bop with horny appeal

One of England's more incongruous customs, the Abbots Bromley Horn Dance is an enchanting timeslip into a bygone age. The cast comprises six local men in dusky red jerkins and green shirts (or vice versa), each carrying a carved deer head affixed with a set of reindeer antlers dating from the 11th century. They are accompanied by a hobbyhorse, a teenage bowman, a Fool and a man dressed as Maid Marian. This hallucinatory troupe wanders the town's houses, farms, pubs and greens from 8am (when the antlers are blessed and collected from their mountings in St Nicholas's Church) till nightfall. The horn-bearers occasionally fall into dual lines or form a circle to dance a series of rudimentary rhythmic steps, advancing, retiring and dipping (never clashing) their horns to the mellifluous melodies of roving squeezebox and triangle players.

First thought to have been performed in 1226 – and variously reported as originating (with scant proof) from pagan fertility rituals, a commemoration of 12th-century hunting rights or a bastardised Morris – the dance remains one of the oldest customs of its kind: an uncanny melding of magical and mundane.

Abbots Bromley, Staffordshire, England
Wakes Monday (early September)

Egremont Crab Fair

Grotesque gurning, ferret shows and apple giveaways

Held annually since 1267, the staging of this convivial gala has been unbroken ever since, save for some pesky wartime years. The fair – established with a Royal Charter by Henry III – was a celebration of the harvest's end, at which the Lord of Egremont gifted crab apples to his serfs. This act is still reflected in the opening Parade of the Apple Carts, with apples tossed from a truck to gathered revellers.

The wider itinerary is endearingly retro. There is Cumberland wrestling, horn blowing, boundary riding, dialect singing, terrier racing, ferret shows and greasy poles to scale (your prize for making it to the top: a side of mutton). Most anticipated of all are the Gurning World Championships – the age-old skill of pulling grotesque faces through a leather horse collar, beloved of the toothless elderly. The lung-busting pipe smoking contest has been sadly curtailed (spoilsports), though an amazing Pathé film from 1969, depicting several old boys huffing like lunatics, is well worth a Google.

Egremont, Cumbria, England
Third Saturday in September

EGREMONT CRAB FAIR.

Braughing Old Man's Day

The spiky legacy of a twice-dead farmer

October of 1571 was either a very good or very bad month for Hertfordshire farmer Mathew Wall. On the one hand, he died. On the other, while his casket was being carried to a freshly dug grave, a pallbearer stumbled on some bracken, jolting Wall awake from his terminal sopor and saving him from a nasty case of premature burial. Wall lived another 24 years; in his 1595 will, he bequeathed a sum of cash to the church sexton to tend his grave (leaving a pile of brambles on it to keep away sheep), as well as requesting an annual tolling of the church bells and payment of a shilling to a local dogsbody to sweep the path.

These demands are still honoured. Every October, a procession begins outside the Golden Fleece pub, where the vicar regales Wall's story. The current resident of the Haven – part of a 17th-century house built on his old land – pays the quid. As funeral bells ring, local primary school children sweep Fleece Lane, brambles are laid and a graveside ditty is sung to commemorate the whole debacle.

Braughing, Hertfordshire, England

2 October

MATHEW WALL
DIED 1595

Punkie Night

Terrifying turnips illuminate Somerset's spookiest night

A creepy rural proxy for the ubiquitous orange pumpkin, 'punkies' are lanterns carved from mangelwurzel beets and turnips, paraded through the streets of this West Somerset village in a ritual dubbed 'Punkie Night'.

The adage goes that, back in the 1800s, the menfolk of Hinton visited a cloth fair in Chiselborough and failed to return on account of getting blind tipsy on ale. Their worried wives went in search, but, lacking oil lamps, had to fashion makeshift lanterns from beets growing in the fields. Seeing the glowing, ghostly, disembodied orbs approaching across the pasture subsequently drove the chaps into a state of wide-eyed terror (the wimps).

These days, children do the roaming, carting their grotesque and intricately carved lamps around the village, led by a Punkie King and Queen, while singing: 'It's punkie night tonight / It's punkie night tonight / Adam and Eve wouldn't believe / It's punkie night tonight.' Their efforts are judged in the church hall and then hung in a field to rot.

Hinton St George, Somerset, England
Last Thursday in October

Samhain and Halloween

Divination and deception mark the onset of winter

Most profoundly associated with the Celtic populace of old Ireland, Scotland and the Isle of Man, Samhain (pronounced 'Sow-wen') was the mystical annual transition from autumn to winter that took place for 24 hours from the evening of 31 October.

This transition to the 'darker half' of the year was believed to be when the veil between the human realm and ghostly 'otherworld' was at its most permeable; a time when giant fires were lit to protect against malevolent spirits, feasts were held and divination games were employed to predict fates, fidelities and fortunes.

There were several adjacent festivals across Britain. Calan Gaeaf in Wales included signature ghosts such as the tailless black sow Hwch Ddu Gwta (occasionally still brought to life by someone dressing in a pig skin and chasing the local children), and a headless lady, Y Ladi Wen. Allantide in Cornwall is held on the liturgical feast day of St Allan, which also includes divination games, while Hop-tu-Naa in the Isle of Man also observed the switch.

Samhain traditions evolved over the centuries, and some feel conspicuously close to today's seasonal hijinks. The practice of 'guising' was first recorded in 16th-century Scotland. This involved adults and children dressing up in costume to confuse vengeful spirits, before visiting houses and reciting verses in exchange for food (and committing mischief if they were rudely denied). Sound familiar?

Some suggest that Samhain morphed into Halloween, though this isn't quite right. Despite the obvious parallels, Halloween actually has its origins in the Christian festival Allhallowtide (commemorating dead saints and martyrs), which wasn't a remotely spooktacular event. During the 8th century, Pope Gregory III shifted the date of Allhallowtide from spring to 1 November – probably in an attempt to Christianise the pre-existing Celtic conventions. Today, the resulting festival, with its focus on the macabre, feels closer to its ancient Celtic predecessor. Old traditions die hard...

Organised community events for Samhain in Britain today are scant, though it remains a time of personal significance for those in tune with Celtic and pagan spirituality. Some mark the occasion by gathering offerings for their forebears or hosting a 'dumb supper', in which an additional place at the table is laid in remembrance of one's dead ancestors.

Halloween shenanigans, of course, are rather more widespread, albeit in rather garish secular forms: from film screenings and club nights to pumpkin picking and ghost-hunting forays around historic houses.

Various locations

31 October – 1 November

Lewes Bonfire

An anarchic conflagration of pyres and puppets

Nestled within the South Downs, Lewes is, for most of the year, a genteel haven of antique shops, art galleries and medieval architecture. Until 5 November, that is, when it becomes a pyrophobic's worst nightmare: a town-wide inferno of raging bonfires and smouldering populist effigies. Active intermittently since the late 1600s, the event commemorates the 1605 Gunpowder Plot (when Guy Fawkes and a host of other peeved Catholics attempted to blow up the Houses of Parliament), and the burning of 17 Protestant martyrs in the mid-1500s. The festival's pervading anti-Catholic sentiment has been dialled down a bit since then.

It's organised by seven anti-authoritarian bonfire societies – two of which, Lewes Borough and Cliffe, were founded way back in 1853. All wear striped smuggler's jumpers in different colours, with white trousers and their own specific sets of 'Pioneer' costumes. The word here is supposed to evoke a sense of defiance or rebellion (rather than having anything to do with the American West), and themes include everything from Vikings, Saxons, Native Americans and Zulus to Cluniac monks, buccaneers, English Civil War soldiers, Yorkists, World War II land girls and child evacuees.

First, 17 burning crosses are carried through the centre to honour the martyrs. Lit barrels are raced along Cliffe High Street, with one thrown into the River Ouse to symbolise a killjoy 18th-century magistrate who tried to ▶

Fire is the name of the game at Lewes's annual pyrotechnic processions

curtail proceedings. The societies walk together in a Grand Procession, holding aloft intricate effigies of politicians, dictators, religious figures and celebrity irritants (a.k.a., the 'Enemies of the Bonfire'). Donald Trump, Kim Jong-Un, Elon Musk, Angela Merkel, David Cameron (holding a marionette of Nick Clegg), Jeremy Clarkson and a number of popes have all been trotted out in years past. Then, it's back to each group's territory for a flame-fuelled knees-up, with each society lighting a huge bonfire and burning their papier-mâché icons.

It's eye-popping stuff: irrefutably Britain's most untethered and anarchic ritual happening. Logistics-wise, it's a pain: local roads are shut and rail services suspended from around 5pm on Bonfire Night until the early hours of the next day, so arrive early and book accommodation well in advance. Even then, the local council begs non-locals to keep away (with zero success).

Lewes, East Sussex, England
5 November (or, if this falls on a Sunday, the preceding Saturday)

Ottery St Mary Tar Barrels

Devon's famous flaming barrels – eyebrows beware

Second to Lewes (p.150), the tar-barrel traditions of this dozy Devon town are Britain's *other* key example of barely constrained conflagrated chaos. Festivities begin with a bang at 5:30am with the unleashing of 'rock cannons' – bent metal pipes with blasting caps, filled with a type of quarrying gunpowder and ignited with a smack from a special hammer. Come evening, wooden barrels slathered with tar and paraffin, each sponsored by a different pub, are lit and hoisted onto the shoulders of a local man, who runs it through the crowd before passing it on (an act that continues until the barrel begins to collapse and is then dropped). Larger barrels with even bigger flames are employed as the evening escalates.

Safety provisions are minimal: participants from families involved in the ritual for generations wear sack-cloth gloves, but that's about it. The barrels used to be rolled, though this practice was deemed too risky and banned in the Victorian era, with scorched hands and tar-spattered faces a 'safer' compromise. The ceremony, wrote photographer Brian Shuel in 1985, remains 'one of the most alarming experiences life has to offer, short of all-out war'.

Ottery St Mary, Devon, England
5 November (or, if this falls on a Sunday, the preceding Saturday)

Turning the Stone

The ritual shifting of a bulky boulder dropped by Satan

Late each autumn, the bell ringers of Shebbear gather at the local church of St Michael's, give an off-key jangle of their instruments, and head, carrying crowbars, to the village green. Here lies the Shebbear Stone, a gargantuan boulder that is ritualistically turned over (with said crowbars) to avoid bad luck for the year ahead.

How the stone got there is up for discussion. Rational minds would say it's an 'erratic': a boulder moved to its current locale by prehistoric glacial erosion. The more romantic might claim it was placed here by Satan, it being a foundation stone for a nearby church that he kept moving to sabotage its completion; or that it was dropped on the devil by St Michael after he was booted from heaven, trapping him beneath – hence having to turn it, damning him to another year underground. Either way, this all explains the name of the local pub: the Devil's Stone Inn.

The folklorist Steve Roud wrote that it is sometimes apocryphally claimed to be England's oldest folk custom – but that there's no recorded proof to suggest it happened much before the 1900s.

Shebbear, Devon, England
5 November

TURN THE
STONE

London Pickle Festival

Pickle paradise in a south London pub

A three-decade staple at Deptford's beloved backstreet boozer, the Dog & Bell, this popular festival is one of south-east London's niftiest modern traditions. Community-led, with local volunteers running the show, it features competitions for the best pickles, preserves, ferments, hot sauces, chutneys, cakes, arts and crafts and photography – think of it as a sort of transplanted Women's Institute shindig for the capital's art school crowd.

Worried you might walk past, unawares? Not to worry: a huge papier-mâché gherkin hangs outside, beckoning in visitors (and the unwitting).

Deptford, London, England
A Saturday in early November

Ackworth Harvest Sheaf

St Cuthbert's Church in Ackworth, a village near Wakefield, is the setting for a sweetly unassuming event in West Yorkshire's folk calendar. After the annual harvest festival service, a tied sheaf of corn is carried from the altar to the church's entrance, over which looms a statue of the titular saint. It's hung over his crozier (a curved religious staff) and left for birdlife to nibble on. The ceremony is extremely low-key – a charming reminder of the methodical and mundane nature of some folk rituals.

Ackworth, West Yorkshire, England
A Sunday in early October

St Martin's Fair and Mock Mayor

Another fake election (see p.84), this time in north Pembrokeshire. As part of the yearly St Martin's Fair (the revival of a medieval winter gala), the villagers walk in old-world garb, holding lanterns, to a 'mayoral seat' on a recumbent boulder on the village green. Speeches and appeals are made in Welsh and English to the incoming mayor, who is then enrolled in their post and celebrated with a steaming bowl of cawl (a Welsh stew).

Trefin, Pembrokeshire, Wales
Usually a weekend in November close to
St Martin's Day (11 November)

Eton Wall Game

Bloody posh schoolboys and impossible goals

A violent, incomprehensible and painstakingly slow sport, the Eton Wall Game has been played at the elite school (alma mater for Tory politicians and royals) since 1776, and is one of Britain's most peculiar perpetuities.

Superficially similar to rugby, it effectively consists of one long scrum – or, as put by a 1948 BBC report, 'an immovable struggle' – played against a 110-metre-long brick wall on a 5-metre-wide pitch. Scoring a single point is rare. Thrown 'goals' – for instance, by hitting a tree at one end of the pitch – are practically impossible.

Teams are fielded by the Scholars (the school's scholarship students) and the Oppidans (the rest, who've paid in). The main event is the annual St Andrew's Day match during Michaelmas term, in which no one has scored since 1909. A true anachronism, it's both fruitless and brutal, with boys being crushed against the wall and routinely bloodied and bruised.

Eton, Berkshire, England
St Andrew's Day (30 November)

Winter

What with factoring in the winter solstice, Christmas, the New Year and Imbolc, the chilliest season is a hotbed of fascinating customs. Invariably, given the plummeting temperatures, there's a whole lot of fire – involving bundles of twigs, torches, barrels of various sizes and anthropomorphised straw bears, among other flammable bits and pieces. There's also a bevy of rough-and-tumble sports games involving great swathes of the populace of several towns and villages, which are, if nothing else, a good way of staying warm.

Holy Thorn Cutting

Transcendental topiary and a gift for the King

With its ethereal tower-topped Tor, and as a site of ley line intersection, the Somerset town of Glastonbury is an esoteric hub. It's also home to a century-old ritual which takes place in the churchyard of St John's, wherein the oldest infant from a local school lops a flowery sprig from a hawthorn tree and sends it to the reigning British monarch for their Christmas lunch table.

The story goes that, way back in antiquity, Joseph of Arimathea (the guy who buried Jesus) visited the town and stuck his staff into the side of Wearyall Hill. It burst into divine flower, and the new tree – a hawthorn – subsequently bloomed twice a year: once as normal in May, and then again at Christmas. That particular tree was chopped down by a Puritan soldier during the English Civil War, but it lived on through some earlier propagations around the town. In 1951, a proper replacement was planted on the hill, but this was again vandalised in 2010. Luckily, two arboreal descendants – which *also* flower biannually – still existed in the churchyard, becoming the source for this pious act of patronage.

Glastonbury, Somerset, England
A schoolday in mid-December

Montol

Errant Osses and an onslaught of sprouts

Launched in 2007, this winter solstice shindig takes its name from the Cornish word for 'balance' – a reference to this threshold of the year, when the days begin to lighten. A town-wide gala of quite startling oddness, there's a hell of a lot to take in.

Kicking off at 2pm, a border troupe of Morris dancers cavorts at Greenmarket, followed by nautically themed guise (costumed) dancing. Then, the gathered groups of revellers (each known as a 'guild') head off to the Farmers Arms for Cornish carols, before two menacing Obby Osses – stylised oilskin-clad hobbyhorses – appear with their minders, pilfering hats from onlookers with their clacking wooden mouths as they amble down Causewayhead, resting at the Star Inn for some hay.

Back at Greenmarket, at 5:40pm a battle occurs between two 10-foot-tall woodsy assailants: the Holly King (who arrives with cries of 'Hoo holly hoo!') and the Oak King, smacking and headbutting each other to retain the privilege of ruling beside the Earth Goddess. The Oak King, as is tradition, always triumphs. To the Celtic strains of a local band, the crowds, now including fire dancers, traipse to a recreation ground, where a huge papier-mâché sun is burned and buried.

By mid-evening, the 'Revels' begin with a vengeance. The 'Gyptians' guild evokes the Gods of Ancient Egypt outside the town's ostentatious Egyptian House, and ►

THE FARMERS ARMS
CAUSEWAYHEAD
Shop, Eat & Enjoy Local

The self-declared 'Chancellor of the Cabbage'

a blitzkrieg of sprout throwing ensues (a tribute to late Falmouth local John Dudding – the self-declared 'Chancellor of the Cabbage', who attended Montol dressed as a giant brassica).

Finally, Tas Nadelik (Cornish Father Christmas) leads a torchlit procession to the sea, where the Lord of Misrule – a kind of archetypal Christmas Fool, chosen from the masked attendees by the drawing of coloured beans – oversees an arcane custom called Chalking the Mock, wherein a chalk figure is drawn on a Yule log and then chucked on a bonfire. The Fool gives a speech, the rest of the sprouts are lobbed at him and everyone dissipates into the night. Got it?

It's a hell of a spectacle and free to attend. Mercifully, the official Montol website has timetables and maps to help visitors catch each bit of the madness.

Penzance, Cornwall, England

Winter solstice (21 December)

Tom Bawcock's Eve

Bad weather means good pie in a Cornish fishing village

The West Penwith harbour village of Mousehole – a couple of miles south of Newlyn and Penzance – might be a bijou spot now but back in the 1500s, it was rather set apart and down on its luck. One year, a shocking bout of weather saw its fishing trade kiboshed, much to the despair of its starving inhabitants. Fortunately, they had a hero in local man Tom Bawcock. A storm raging around him, he headed into the squall and single-handedly landed a miraculous catch, feeding everyone in the village.

These days, his derring-do is commemorated with an atmospheric parade of paper lanterns – the conical, illuminated constructions sweetly decorated with illustrations of fish and stars. It's followed by a slap-up feast of 'stargazy pie' – silvery sardine heads poking out from its burnished pastry lid, peering up at the cosmos – at the Ship Inn on the village harbour.

Mousehole, Cornwall, England

23 December

Ringing the Devil's Knell

Persistent pealing on the eve of Christmas

A sonorous endurance test with few parallels, this bell-ringing exercise has darker origins than usual joyful peals heralding Christmastide. Come 10pm at Dewsbury Minster, a 1.2-metre-wide tenor bell (dubbed Black Tom) is rung for every year since the birth of Jesus, all timed so that the final big bong happens dead on the stroke of midnight. Each ringer takes it in turn to do 100 pulls. The meticulously timed 'funeral pace' is maintained by tower captain Derek Johnstone, aided by an electronic counter and some geometric paper charts.

Legend has it that the marathon ringing was inaugurated by the 15th-century Thomas de Soothill, a local knight who murdered a servant boy by shoving him into a lake. As penance, he bequeathed the bell and asked that it be rung each year – though it's also thought that it may have started as a means of reminding the parish of the death of Satan on Christ's birthday. Either way, this melodious memento fell out of fashion for eons, until its revival in 1828: the bells have chimed ever since.

Dewsbury, West Yorkshire, England

Christmas Eve

Newburgh Oddfellows Parade

A backwards procession on a humungous horse

Odd by name, palpably crackers in action, this seasonal curio is largely unknown outside of its hometown, a royal burgh (borough) on the Firth of Tay's lower shore. A pre-Hogmanay celebration, it was first held in 1885 and organised by the titular Oddfellows, an international fraternal society of which Newburgh's is the only active Scottish 'lodge'. The bizarre torchlit procession begins outside the Steeple Town House. An 'Apprentice' – one of the newest local lodge initiates – dons a double-sided mask (facing both towards the new year and away from the outgoing one) and rides backwards on a huge Clydesdale horse through the streets.

An eerie cohort of disguised figures follows – wearing anything from Halloween-style pig, skull and werewolf masks to medieval knight, serf and priest costumes – menacing onlookers, stealing hats and plucking up children as they go. Sounds malevolent, sure, but in practice it's all very convivial, with attendees knocking back drams of whisky to the sound of the accompanying brass band.

Newburgh, Fife, Scotland

New Year's Eve

Kirkwall Ba'

Uppies and Doonies play a warped take on football

Wild rough-and-tumble mischief on the northern Scottish archipelago, the Ba' is yet another transmutation of the chaotic medieval 'mob' football. Twice over the festive period, the shop windows and doors of Kirkwall are boarded up in anticipation of the game. There are no rules as such, but the premise is simple: at 1pm, a black and rust-red leather ball (the titular ba', a new version of which is made each year) is thrown from the stone cross standing beneath the steeple of St Magnus Cathedral, into a gargantuan throng of locals. Then, a team of 'Uppies' (whose fathers were born north of the cross) and a team of 'Doonies' (you guessed it, south of the cross) form a humungous, grinding scrum around the ball, trying to force it to their respective goals. For the Uppies, that's a mundane gable wall beneath a sign pointing to Orphir, by the old town gates; for the Doonies it's the harbour (whoever wants to claim it for themselves must jump in after it).

The team members usually number into the hundreds and are not visually distinguished from each other. Players don old clothes, remove watches and even reinforce their legs and arms with gaffer tape. Things get demonstrably more intense as the scrum reaches the narrower streets and night falls (though proceedings do pause if anyone faints, and people are quick on their feet when the scrum turns, to avoid getting squished). The ba' must be moved through non-mechanical means – but it's considered fair game to ▶

stick it up one's shirt and attempt to smuggle it to the goals.

The longest recorded men's Ba' game (in 1975) lasted seven hours; the shortest (in 1952) a cool four minutes. When the ba' does finally reach a goal, an individual winner is then picked from the triumphant team by way of *another* scrummage, involving longstanding players or those who particularly excelled themselves that year. The ball is repaired, varnished and displayed with beaming pride in the home of the victor – a rare accolade of utmost significance for folk of this proud island community.

Kirkwall, Orkney, Scotland
Christmas Day and New Year's Day (or, if either falls on a Sunday, the following day)

Old Time Paper Boys

Father Christmas heralds a mummers' play for the ages

Originating in the Middle Ages, mumming has been intermittently omnipresent around Christmas – in basically all counties apart from Norfolk and Suffolk, for some reason. It involves performing rudimentary combat plays on village greens, town squares and pub forecourts across the land. Each group plies its own idiosyncratic riffs on the narrative, but the basic plot sees a protagonist (often a King or St George) duel with a nefarious assailant (such as a Turkish Knight or the 'Bold Slasher'), with interjections from side roles including a doctor and various other county-specific characters.

Revived in the 1930s by a local vicar and his sister, Marshfield's mummers group, the Old Time Paper Boys, is one of the country's more distinctive ensembles – largely due to the wackadoodle costumes, comprised of thousands of strips of paper (hence the name). Every Boxing Day, the town crier arrives at the marketplace at 11am to herald the arrival of the Boys. Then, Father Christmas (bedecked in red strips) emerges to declare, 'Plum pudding and mince pie! Who likes that better than King William and I?' before introducing the sword-wielding Little Man John, who challenges those around him to 'Cut me and slay me as small as dust – send me to Jamaica, to be made into mince pie crust!'

King William steps up with his spear, reels off some lines about killing a fiery dragon and, after some clashing of wooden swords, strikes John down. Enter Doctor Jack ►

A performer from the Old Time Paper Boys, a mummers group known for its striking paper-draped costumes

Phoenix, who offers his medical bona fides and resurrects John using a bottle of turps (for a mere £15).

Next up is Saucy Jack (with 'his wife and family at his back', in the form of some dolls tied to his garb); then Tenpenny Nick ('the biggest rough amongst you all'); and Old Father Beelzebub, brandishing a club and a money pan, which he shakes for donations. It culminates with the troupe monotonously singing a three-verse song while walking around in a circle, before heading off to do the whole thing again at various other locales, with the last performance being at midday.

It's really quite odd: simultaneously low-key, mesmerising and very English, all performed in a kind of laconic recitation with little thespian energy. As with all mummers' plays, the script has been passed through the generations orally – 'garbled into doggerel nonsense without ever quite losing their underlying sense of ritual purpose', as the BBC's 1977 folk documentary, *Here We Come A Wassailing* put it – and it remains one of the most fascinatingly esoteric curios of the folk calendar.

Marshfield, Gloucestershire, England

Boxing Day

Sword Dancing

Cutting-edge capers in an ancient armed dance

Native to Yorkshire, Northumberland and Durham, sword danĉing is a form of mumming, though not as ubiquitous as the combat play seen around many a pub and market square this time of year. A group of dancers each holds a 'sword' (actually a wooden stick or metal lath) and performs a series of perfunctory steps before linking them in a tight, overlaid pattern of a knot or star, which is then held aloft. As with many strange heritage happenings, it's anecdotally ancient but most likely dates to the 1750s (having ebbed before a 20th-century revival).

A few notable groups still uphold the tradition. Clad in sky-blue and pink, North Yorkshire's Goathland Plough Stots hold their signature 'Day of Dance' on Plough Monday (the first Monday after Epiphany), ambling the village to perform one of five trademark turns, accompanied by a Fool, a gaggle of musicians and a miniature plough. Similarly sharp are the Redcar Sword Dancers, decked out in cherry-red military regalia, who prance at Greatham, County Durham, while Flamborough in the East Riding and Grenoside in South Yorkshire both boast established ensembles.

Various locations
Around Christmas and into January

Wassailing

Cider-soaked hullabaloos in the orchards of England

Wassailing is a fruity rural ceremony with deep pagan roots, originally tied to Twelfth Night on 5 January or Old Twelfth Night on 17 January – the latter date preserved from the Julian calendar.

In the days of old, apple-growing communities (especially around the West Country, Sussex and Kent) would steel themselves for the dark, freezing, agriculturally barren months following Christmas by hailing hearty toasts to the trees in their orchards, as a means of encouraging fertility, abundance and the warding off of evil spirits. As night fell, the folk would make for the orchards with gallons of cider, bread, pots, pans and even shotguns. Locating a particularly bountiful tree, they'd sprinkle it with cider, hang slices of toast from its branches, make a godawful ballyhoo with the kitchenware and occasionally blast their shotguns into the canopy – all to shoo away the malevolent ghosts that might stymy the new year's harvest. (In Devon, it's reported that a young boy would sometimes be raised into the foliage shouting 'Tit! Tit! More to eat!' though he'd be safely lowered before any firearms went off.)

Afterwards, a steaming bowl of mulled cider laced with seasonal spices like nutmeg and cloves would be passed around for the shivering denizens to sup from. Throughout, toasts of 'Wassail!' would be met with replies of 'Drink hail!' and choruses of the banger 'Wassailer's Carol' belted out. Way back when, the low months really would have ►

been miserable, so the ritual was a neat way of wresting some assumed control over nature's erratic whims (and an excuse to get a little tipsy). There was also a second, house-visiting form of the archaic wassail, wherein revellers would go door-to-door around villages and isolated farmhouses, proffering the boozy bowl, but this was largely superseded by carolling.

Given the modern proliferation of revived folk traditions, wassailing now abounds anew. Many big-name cider makers hold wassails (Westons in Herefordshire and Thatchers in Somerset among 'em). On a less brand-centric level, Stroud's major 2014 revival, held at the Museum in the Park, is a vibey bustle of cider slurping, Morris dancing and dramatic appearances of the Broad (the town's version of a hobbyhorse), who chases locals out of their houses. In London, umpteen community orchards stage their own woozy gatherings, in neighbourhoods as far afield as Walthamstow, Barnes Common, Blythe Hill and Bermondsey.

Various: everywhere apples are grown

Late December till February

Stromness Yule Log Pull

Tree-based tug of war in the Northern Isles

Not content with a regular tug of war, the people of Stromness have long given theirs a wooden twist. Traditionally taking place on Christmas Eve, but now moved to New Year's Eve, a din of airhorns announces the beginning of the log pull. Cheered on by crowds, locals from either end of town (collectively known as 'Northenders' and 'Soothenders') strain to haul a hefty log affixed with ropes 200 metres from Graham Place, either to Pierhead (for the Norths) or Ma Humph's Pier (for the Sooths), with great yells of 'Heave!' as they go.

The log is donated by a sawmill but used to be pilfered from an unsuspecting resident's garden by nightfall – arboreal skulduggery that saw people camping out to protect their trees until the custom was banned by the town council in 1935. A replacement log was provided by the municipality for the next few years, but the log pull fell out of fashion in 1937 and was thankfully revived 80 years later. The main adults' contest kicks off at 4:30pm, but there's a junior version for the bairns – with a smaller tree – at 2:30pm.

Stromness, Orkney, Scotland
New Year's Eve

Allendale Tar Bar'l

More burning barrels, with added brass bands

Also known as the Bahl, Bah'l or Baal (you get the picture), this northern proxy to the flaming procession down in Devon's Ottery St Mary (p.154) might be somewhat less chaotic, but it's still a dramatic occurrence. Forty-five plucky Allendale men – faces sooted and in colourful garb – run around the village with flaming wooden barrels perched on their heads. The barrels are, in fact, hacked-down versions of regular wooden ones, approximately 30 centimetres in depth (though still weighing about 13 kilograms), filled with wood shavings and bits of cloth, all soaked in paraffin.

As with many of the customs in this book, its origins are unreliably linked back to medieval times, though it's more likely to have originated in the mid-19th century, possibly as a means of illuminating the way for the brass band that still marches alongside the blazing buckets. The hot, parping procession reaches the village's Market Place at the stroke of midnight for a big old bonfire and a rousing chorus of 'Auld Lang Syne.'

Allendale, Northumberland, England

New Year's Eve

Flaming paraffin-soaked barrels are carried overhead at the Allendale Tar Bar'l

Twelfth Night

A Green Man and St George rejoice by the Thames

The Christmas season is given a particularly lurid send-off on London's South Bank. Organised by the Lions part theatre company and staged outside Shakespeare's Globe, it features a full gamut of esoteric midwinter characters.

Foremost is the Holly Man, cold-weather guise of the folkloric staple of the Green Man – a verdant fever dream of pine, ivy and holly – played by David Risley for over 30 years. Carried over the Thames by boat, he 'brings the green', symbolising the imminent arrival of fecund new growth. He's led by the London Beadle (an elected official) to a tootling, jangling soundtrack, then joined by some mummers to hold a toast and wassail.

The crowds then head to the jetty for a technicolour rendition of the St George's combat play. The characters of St George and Turkey Sniper (a bastardisation of the classic Turkish Knight) are joined by extras like Father Christmas, Clever Leggs and the Old Oss.

At the end, cakes are presented to onlookers; whosoever finds a bean or pea in their slice is crowned King Bean or Queen Pea and danced along the riverside to Soap Yard for more singing, storytelling, the heralding of a 'Kissing Wishing' tree and as much mulled wine as you can quaff.

Bankside, London, England
Sunday closest to Twelfth Night (6 January)

Twelfth Night celebrations on London's South Bank, featuring the Holly Man and other notable midwinter characters

Haxey Hood

A wayward rugby match featuring a batch of Boggins

Every Epiphany, villagers from Haxey and Westwoodside in the Isle of Axholme (so called as it was once surrounded by wetlands, now drained) meet in teams to play an unfathomable sports match. The objective is to capture and transport a tightly rolled tube of leather (the 'hood') to one of two goals, the doorways of each respective team's home pub: the Carpenters Arms in Westwoodside; the Kings Arms in Haxey. The game is presided over by a Lord of the Hood, a Chief Boggin (both wear floral headdresses), another ten regular Boggins (in red jackets) and a Fool (in a jacket covered in shreds of cloth). The Lord (carrying a wand of 13 willow sticks) and Boggins convene for an ale-sloshing pub crawl, where they paint the Fool's face red and black.

Heading towards the church, the Fool attempts to escape but is quickly caught by the Boggins and wrangled to the base of an old cross outside Haxey church. Here, he makes an inscrutable speech to the watching crowd, before the Boggins light a straw fire to 'smoke him' as a form of purification. When the smoke gets a bit much, the Fool signals the procession to nearby Haxey Hill and the game begins. But first, there's the 'Running Hood': a preamble frolic whereby the Lord throws 12 sackcloth hoods into the air in succession, grabbed by participants (mostly local youths) who try and escape the field without being tagged by a Boggin. ►

The 'hood' – a tightly rolled tube of leather – is the prized item in this frenzied rugby match

An hour before sunset, it's time for the main event. The leather hood is thrown into the air; whoever catches it is then engulfed in a giant scrum – the 'sway' – which moves, at a glacial pace over a matter of hours, towards one of the pubs. When it's forced through the threshold by the hundreds-strong huddle, the boozer's boss touches it and it's game over, the hood then displayed proudly behind the bar for the following year.

The Hood's origins are somewhat foggy; a common tale is that the historic Lady de Mowbray had her hat blown off in a gust, which was then chased down in a calamitous style by 13 fieldhands. This so amused Lord de Mowbray that he donated a tract of land to perform a reprisal of the whole slapstick scene each year. Very likely a fabricated yarn and, in any case, its earliest known recording was in 1815 (though some say it was played as far back as the 1300s).

Isle of Axholme, Lincolnshire, England
Twelfth Night (6 January; or, if this falls on a Sunday, the preceding Saturday)

Burning the Ashen Faggot

Flame-cracked withies in a West Country pub

This peculiar West Country riff on wassailing and Yule log traditions sees a small, bound bundle of ash sticks, known as a 'faggot', incinerated to an enthusiastic rendition of Exmoor's 'Dunster Carol'.

The faggot burned at Laymore's Squirrel Inn is of a particularly maniacal size. For years, a local chap called Mike has constructed faggots 12 feet in length, made in part with the half-burned remnants of the previous year's and tied with 12 green strips of ash (known as 'withies'). One end of this is placed in the lit pub hearth and must be intermittently shoved further in as it smoulders. When a withy snaps, a toast is drunk, bets are placed on how long it'll take to burn and there's a buffet supper to boot. It's also believed that any woman who steps over the smouldering bundle will be expecting within a year.

Genesis-wise, some believe that faggot burning has links to the Saxons – one of the many pagan curios absorbed into the Christian seasonal programme to further exert the church's influence over rural life.

Laymore, Dorset, England
Twelfth Night (6 January)

Selkirk Haggis Hunt

Polka-fuelled pursuit of petite offal parcels

This Borders town perpetuates a puckish yearly 'hunt' for wild haggis – fictitious badger-like creatures said to be the source of haggis (yes, that palatable parcel of steamed sheep's stomach stuffed with offal, oats and white pepper). Ahead of the ubiquitous Scottish Burns Night celebrations, hordes of locals – as many as 400 some years, armed with small nets and soft sticks – march from the town centre to Selkirk Hill, stopping halfway to dance to a 'haggis polka' performed by a local fiddle group, before being led up the slopes by a lone piper. The reedy strains of the bagpipes are said to help flush the haggis from their burrows, which are then netted, bagged and carried to a hilltop hut, where Rabbie Burns's poetic address is recited and a haggis cooked and shared out. To be clear, no real haggis are harmed; these are only knitted haggis created and hidden by local volunteers.

As localised ceremonies go, it's charmingly weird, oddly low-key and invariably whisky-fuelled. It's also a fine example of the longstanding Scottish insistence that the haggis is a living creature, epitomised by the Haggis Wildlife Foundation. On its website, expect to see footage of furry haggis bobbing in the sea and waking from hibernation – a joyous use of AI, if not one's time.

Selkirk, Scottish Borders, Scotland
Sunday before Burns Night (25 January)

Burning of the Clavie

Lucky sticks and a burning beacon

Another Caledonian fire festival, Burghead's sees the titular 'clavie' – a flaming barrel of creosote and kindling – walked through the town before being burned in a bonfire on Doorie Hill.

The receptacle itself is half a whisky barrel held together with iron hoops, attached to a holding post with a single nail (the same one is used every year), knocked in with a stone. It's then secured with several other staves – a kind of miniature, movable beacon. After being lit with a chunk of smouldering peat, it's carried from the home of the Clavie King – longtime builder of the clavie, and a hereditary role – and hoisted along by a succession of local men, known as 'Brochers'. Stopping at a number of preordained houses to pay tribute and hand over a burning stick from the barrel to light their hearths, it eventually reaches an old fort on the hillside. Here, more fuel is added and the whole lot is burned to ashes, with onlookers often nabbing cold embers to nail above their doors, horseshoe-style, for good luck.

Burghead, Moray, Scotland

11 January (or, if this falls on a Sunday, the preceding Saturday)

Whittlesea Straw Bear Festival

Ursine madness in the midst of the Fens

The wildly horizontal levels of the Cambridgeshire Fens – specifically the damp tracts around the village of Whittlesey – are the site of a strange, ursine ceremony in the parading of the 'straw bear'. First recorded across the region in the 1850s, it now sees a cohort of locals led through the streets in huge, cumbersome costumes of straw (more akin to monstrously sentient hay bales than bears), followed by troupes of Morris and Molly dancers, and a gaggle of Plough Boys pulling a decorated plough. These straw behemoths are cast off and burned at a nearby fish farm at the close: ritual benefaction to the new planting and inaugural ploughing of spring.

The tradition faded away with the onset of World War I, at which point it was rather frowned upon as a form of 'cadging' – the 'bears' being made to jig around for money outside posher residences and thus banned in some of the other villages – but it was revived in Whittlesey (in this cashless form) in 1980.

Whittlesey, Cambridgeshire, England
Second or third week in January

Chepstow Wassail and Mari Lwyd

Skeletal horses and steaming cider

Chepstow's folk gala is a ghostly clashing of ancient and modern on the riverside border of England and Wales. It is notable for an appearance of the formidable Mari Lwyd, a haggard South Wales take on the hobbyhorse, with a bleached horse's skull (complete with articulated, clattering jaw and shimmering bauble eyes) carried on a pole, its bearer hidden beneath a sheet.

The parade of the mare is convivial and faintly nightmarish, led through the town by amassed revellers, Morris men and a decorated apple cart to the bridge over the Wye, where Welsh and English contingents meet and sidle back to the Chepstow Museum. Here, the horse and its handlers attempt to gain entry to the building by way of outlandish back-and-forth verses spoken in both languages ('Go away! Outside my door rattling, you old monkey, with your stinking breath. And stop your prattling!') Afterwards, a wassail is compered and a steaming, communal cider bowl passed around, received with boozy glee by the gathered crowds. It's a bananas sight – a sweetly unsettling blurring of life and death, deserving of the enthusiastic revival seen since the mid-20th century.

Chepstow, Monmouthshire, Wales
Last Saturday in January

Up Helly Aa

A Viking-themed fire festival of historic renown

Perhaps *the* iconic iteration of the traditional Scottish fire festival, Lerwick's infernal gathering is a celebration of the region's Norse Viking heritage. It's a bit hard to follow, so pay attention. Basically, various squads of guizers (the catch-all term for participants) march through the town, led by the Jarl (a principal guizer whose group is known as the Jarl Squad), before an elaborately ornate, life-size Viking galley is burned.

It all kicks off early doors, with the Jarl Squad meandering through Lerwick (galley in tow) to the Market Cross, where the 'Guizer's Bill' – a dense painted sign filled with puzzling stories, lyrics, odd skits and jokes – details in irreverent form the proceedings of the day. They then head to the town hall for an invitation-only civic reception, where the Jarl is given the symbolic 'freedom of the town' for 24 hours, before continuing on to the Shetland Museum for 3pm (at which point the public can attend and eyeball all the shiny Viking regalia).

After a junior procession, cheered on by the adult squads, the Jarl Squad marches through the other groups to assume its place at the front of the main parade. At 7:30pm, the 'lighting up' is signalled: an eyebrow-singeing spectacle of over 900 hessian fuel-soaked torches, set alight and filling the winter night with roaring flame and smoke. The whole movable conflagration is then led by the Jarl, resplendent at the front of the galley, to the ►

King George V playing field, where the ship is incinerated in a ritual out of sight of the public.

It's a crazy feat of preparation, the squads clad in arduously crafted garb, with helmets and shields of their own making (the designing of which begins ages before). The galley itself is a bona fide work of art: made to a design from 1949 and overseen by local boat-builder James 'Boatie Jeemie' Smith, it measures 9.2 metres long and 3.5 metres tall at the top of its snarling dragon masthead and a full 6 metres tall at the mast's tip.

Save a few fallow years – for wars, plagues, flu and the deaths of Queen Victoria, George V and Winston Churchill – it's been an integral Shetland calendar fixture since originating in the 1880s and shows no sign of petering out.

Lerwick, Shetland, Scotland
Last Tuesday in January

Marsden Imbolc Fire Festival

Fireside battling giants and masked dancing

The midpoint between the winter solstice and the vernal equinox, Imbolc is an important Gaelic/neopagan festival marking the early arrival of spring, and one of the four ancient Celtic seasonal transitions (along with Beltane, Lughnasadh and Samhain). In Ireland, it's now conflated with the feast day of St Brigid, associated with fertility, holy wells and new birth.

Britain has a few Imbolc celebrations of its own, not least the prosaically named Imbolc Fire Festival at Marsden in West Yorkshire. Founded in 1990, it includes various arcane elements, including the wearing of animal masks (a harkening back to the traditional tendency for guising) and flaming torch processions, as well as a symbolic scuffle between the Green Man and Jack Frost, his icy adversary. The foliaged giant always prevails, driving out the chill of winter and welcoming the blossoming warmth of spring.

Marsden, West Yorkshire, England
First Saturday in February; every other year

Hunting the Mallard

Inaugurated in 1632 but now held once a century (the next is in 2101), this oddball foray sees Fellows from the historic All Souls College elect a 'Lord Mallard' from their ranks, who is then raised and carried around the grounds in a torch-lit procession to 'hunt' the titular (and entirely fictitious) waterfowl. He's accompanied on his drunken chase by six 'officers' – all wearing medals adorned with pictures of mallards, and one holding a wooden duck on a stick – while singing a mallard-themed song. Students, eh?

Oxford, Oxfordshire, England
14 January; every 100 years

Calan Hen

The traditional Welsh ringing in of the Old New Year has been held annually for two centuries. At St Tysul's church in Llandysul, readings from the Welsh Bible are followed by children scuttling between houses, opportunistically cooing '*Blwyddyn Newydd dda i chi*' ('A happy new year to you') in exchange for gifts of cash and sweets, known as *calennig*. Everyone then gathers for a hearty Welsh feast.

Llandysul, Ceredigion, Wales
Second Saturday in January

Grimaldi Clown Service

Death is no laughing matter – but don't tell that to the many and assorted clowns who descend on Haggerston's All Saints Church each year. Professional and amateur laugh-merchants alike, bedecked in multicoloured regalia and face paint, congregate to make a prayer to 'the precious gift of laughter' in honour of the Englishman Joseph Grimaldi – who, along with archetypal 'sad clown' Pierrot, was responsible for much of what we know of the clowning tradition. Funny old life – though anyone afflicted with chromophobia should avoid like the plague.

Haggerston, London, England
First Sunday in February

Slaithwaite Moonraking

The story goes that, while retrieving a barrel of hooch from the Huddersfield Canal, some 19th-century booze smugglers were apprehended by excise men. They feigned drunkenness and claimed that the moon had fallen in and they were trying to 'rake it out' – ingenuity remembered with a yearly canalside parade of lanterns made from tissue and willow. A huge, illuminated moon is floated in a boat alongside, eventually hoisted out of the water with a cherry picker and returned to the night sky.

Slaithwaite, West Yorkshire, England
A Saturday in late February; every other year

Hurling the Silver Ball

Cornwall's quirkiest beach-based take on basketball

Hurling is a game unique to Cornwall (entirely distinct from the Irish sport with which it coincidentally shares a name) in which a ball – fist-sized, made of cork or wood and painted silver – is hoofed by hand between two goals by teams of indeterminate sizes over sprawling stretches of land. It's still played every year at the beach at St Ives, largely by the town's youth, to mark the 1434 consecration of the church of St Ia. At 9:30am, the mayor – ward of the ball for the rest of the year – produces the hallowed orb and blesses it in the well (or *venton*) of St Ia, before tossing it onto the Porthmeor sands below. The congregated players exclaim, 'Fair play is good play!' and the teams – from either 'uplong' or 'downlong' the town, though it's thought that one was once comprised only of chaps called Tom, Will or John – win points by aiming the ball through two nets, with everything ceasing at noon.

Hurling has been reported across the county as far back as the 1580s; indeed, the immaculate stone circle of The Hurlers, about 100 kilometres east near Minions, was so named after an apocryphal band of players turned to stone for heretically hurling on the sabbath.

St Ives, Cornwall, England
First Monday after 3 February

Boar's Head Ceremony

A gory gift to the Lord Mayor of London

Back in 1343, a stink was brewing in the Shambles, a parish just southeast of London's illustrious Smithfield Market. The neighbourhood's butchers had taken to throwing their gory, offaly detritus in the street, perturbing the wandering monks of nearby Greyfriars. As a solution, the then Lord Mayor – aptly named John Hammond – granted the butchers a plot of land next to the fetid River Fleet in which to dispose of the assorted viscera and entrails. The price? An annual gift of a boar's head to the generous dignitary.

Nowadays, the land is gone but the tradition continues (sort of, anyway). Each year, following a private sausage lunch at Butchers' Hall in Bartholomew Close, the ancient Worshipful Company of Butchers – one of London's oldest Livery Companies, dating back to 975 CE – congregates in fur-trimmed blue robes and marches to Mansion House via Cheapside. The parade is led by a Beadle and pipers, and its star is a wonderful red papier-mâché model of a boar's head – its mouth stuffed with an orange – to present to the expectant mayor. Word has it that a real boar's head precedes, to be scoffed by City bigwigs out of the gaze of the proles.

City of London, London, England
Early February to April (though varies)

H&M
M&S FOOD
BOSS

Further Resources

Books

Charles Hardwick, *Traditions, superstitions, and folklore: chiefly Lancashire and the north of England* (1872)

Christina Hole, *A Dictionary of British Folk Customs* (Paladin, 1978)

Christina Hole, *British Folk Customs* (Hutchinson, 1976)

Jennifer Westwood and Jacqueline Simpson, *Lore of the Land: A Guide to England's Myths and Legends* (Penguin, 2005)

Julia Bishop and Steve Roud, *The New Penguin Book of English Folk Songs* (Penguin, 2014)

Lally MacBeth, *The Lost Folk: From the Forgotten Past to the Emerging Future of Folk* (Faber & Faber, 2025)

Mark Norman, *Britain's Folklore Year* (National Trust, 2025)

Michael Howard, *Sacred Ring: Pagan Origins of British Folk Festivals & Customs* (Capall Bann, 1995)

Sheila Livingstone, *Scottish Festivals* (Birlinn, 2025)

Steve Roud, *The English Year* (Penguin, 2008)

T. Gwynn Jones, *Welsh Folklore and Folk Custom* (originally published 1930; Cockatrice Books, 2020)

Weird Walk, *Weird Walk: Wanderings and Wonderings Through the British Ritual Year* (Watkins, 2023)

Zakia Sewell, *Finding Albion: Myth, Folklore and the Quest for a Hidden Britain* (Hodder Press, 2026)

Films & TV

Arcadia (dir. Paul Wright; Hopscotch Films, Crossover and Common Ground, 2017)

The Archivist: Adventures in Time & Space & Folklore (dirs. Rob Curry and Tim Plester; Fifth Column Films, Tyke Films and Weird Walk, 2026)

Charlie Cooper's Myth Country (BBC, 2024)

Escape to River Cottage; *Return to River Cottage*; *River Cottage Forever* (Keo Films, 1999, 2000, 2002)

Here We Come A Wassailing (BBC Bristol, 1977)

BBC Archive (which includes a plethora of amazing old films on British folk rituals)

Websites & Organisations

Calendar Customs (calendarcustoms.com)

Circle Dance (@circledancerecs)

English Folk Dance and Song Society at Cecil Sharp House (efdss.org/cecil-sharp-house)

The Museum of English Rural Life, Reading (merl.reading.ac.uk)

Offbeat Folk Film Club (offbeat.film)

Stone Club (stoneclub.rocks)

All thanks to Dulcie, Ruby, Vince, Ally, Andrew, Ivy, Rosie, Ju, Amelia, Basil, Philip and Emma, Agnes and Paula at Country Life for tolerating the endless prattling on about various aspects of this book. As ever, thanks too to Flo, Dom, Olivia, Martin and Ann at Hoxton Mini Press for their wonderful editing, design and continued support in my rambling pursuit of the culturally esoteric.

Tom Howells

Tom Howells is a journalist and editor who has written for *Country Life*, *The Financial Times*, *Vogue*, *The Guardian*, *World of Interiors*, *Slop*, *The Quietus*, *FACT*, *MacGuffin*, *The Fence*, *Wallpaper** and more. Though he hails from the Isle of Wight, he's never visited Bramble Bank and feels a complete fraud for it (though his cricket skills are subpar, in any case).

Hoxton Mini Press

Hoxton Mini Press is a small independent publisher based in east London. We are committed to making beautiful but affordable books that don't screw up the planet. We offset all our printing, and we hope that the trees we do use will continue their life as beautiful books that you'll pass on to your grandchildren.

Page 14 © Livvi Grant; Page 15 © Livvi Grant; Page 16 © Guy Corbishley / Alamy; Page 18 © Eddie Keogh / Reuters; Page 20 © Livvi Grant; Page 21 © Alex Kurunis; Olney Pancake Race © Carl Court; Alnwick Shrovetide Football Match © PA Images / Alamy; Jethart Hand Ba' © Jeff J Mitchell; Hare Pie Scramble and Bottle Kicking © Haydn Denman; Pace Egging Plays © Rory Prior / Alamy; Beltane Fire Festival © Andy Buchanan / Alamy; Padstow Obby Oss first image © Mike Greenslade / Alamy, second image © Education Images; Hastings Jack in the Green © Alex Kurunis; Blackawton International Festival of Worm Charming © PA Images / Alamy; Helston Flora Day © David Hastilow / Alamy; Whitby Penny Hedge © Ian Forsyth; Tissington Well Dressing © Oscar Hill; Beating the Bounds © Chrysoulla Rosling / Alamy; High Wycombe Mayor Weigh-In © D. Callcut / Alamy; Cooper's Hill Cheese-Rolling first image © Cameron Smith, second and third images © Livvi Grant; Tetbury Woolsack Races © Terry Mathews / Alamy; Bampton Morris Dance © Jason Hornblow / Alamy; Hunting of the Earl of the Rone © Robert Harding / Alamy; Robert Dover's Olimpick Games © Nick Turner / Alamy; Castleton Garland Day © Dan Kitwood; Great Wishford's Oak Apple Day © Haydn Wheeler / Alamy; Maldon Mud Race © PA Images / Alamy; Hawick Common Riding first image © David Fernie / Alamy, second image © Emma Wood / Alamy; Mayor of Ock Street © Chris Honeywell / Alamy; Glastonbury Festival © PA Images / Alamy; Summer Solstice © Livvi Grant; World Nettle Eating Championship © Finnbarr Webster; Whalton Baal Fire © Linsey Saxon; Sma' Shot Day © Skully / Alamy; Grasmere Rushbearing © Picturebank / Alamy; World Peashooting Championship © Julian Eales / Alamy; Swan Upping first image © The Washington Post, second image © Dan Kitwood; Bread Ahead Lammas Day © Bread Ahead; The Burryman Procession © Alex Kurunis; Knighthood of the Old Green © Homer Sykes / Alamy; Kilwinning Papingo Shoot © Arkley Simpson; Aberaeron Mackerel Fiesta © Andrew Chittock / Alamy; World Bog Snorkelling Championship © Emma Wood / Alamy; Bramble Bank Cricket Match © Popperfoto; Braemar Highland Gathering © Michael Dunlea / Alamy; World Stone Skimming Championships © Jeff J Mitchell; Sowerby Bridge Rushbearing © PA Images / Alamy; Marldon Apple Pie Fair © Andy Styles Photography / Alamy; Abbots Bromley Horn Dance © Christopher Furlong; Egremont Crab Fair © Rod Edwards / Alamy; Braughing Old Man's Day © Homer Sykes / Alamy; Punkie Night © Livvi Grant; Lewes Bonfire first image © Glyn Kirk, second image © Mike Kemp; Ottery St Mary Tar Barrels © Nicholas Bragger; Turning the Stone © Carole Evans; Eton Wall Game © Christopher Furlong; Holy Thorn Cutting © Third Cross / Alamy; Montol first image © Gordon Scammell / Alamy, second image © Natasha Quarmby / Alamy; Tom Bawcock's Eve © Simon Maycock / Alamy; Kirkwall Ba' © Jeff J Mitchell; Old Time Paper Boys © Matt Cardy; Sword Dancing © zcbill / Alamy; Wassailing © Livvi Grant; Allendale Tar Bar'l © PA Images; Twelfth Night first image © Jeff Gilbert / Alamy, second image © SOPA Images; Haxey Hood © Christopher Furlong; Burning of the Clavie © Jeff J Mitchell; Whittlesea Straw Bear Festival © Homer Sykes / Alamy; Chepstow Wassail and Mari Lwyd © David Broadbent / Alamy; Up Helly Aa first image © Andy Buchanan, second image © Euan Cherry; Marsden Imbolc Fire Festival © Oli Scarff; Hurling the Silver Ball © Simon Maycock / Alamy; Boar's Head Ceremony © Stephen Chung / Alamy.

Events by Region

Scotland Highlands & Islands

Birnam World Haggis-Eating Championship, 124
Braemar Highland Gathering, 132
Burning of the Clavie, 200
Kirkwall Ba', 174
Stromness Yule Log Pull, 186
Up Helly Aa, 206
World Stone Skimming Championships, 134

Scotland Lowlands

Beltane Fire Festival, 38
Hawick Common Riding, 80
Jethart Hand Ba', 28
Kilwinning Papingo Shoot, 120
Newburgh Oddfellows Parade, 173
Selkirk Haggis Hunt, 199
Sma' Shot Day, 96
The Burryman Procession, 114
Whuppity Scoorie, 28

Wales

Aberaeron Mackerel Fiesta, 122
Calan Hen, 212
Chepstow Wassail and Mari Lwyd, 204
Cilgerran Coracle Races, 117
National Eisteddfod of Wales, 110
St Martin's Fair and Mock Mayor, 159
Throwing the Feat Stone, 131
World Bog Snorkelling Championships, 124

North England

Ackworth Harvest Sheaf, 159
Allendale Tar Bar'l, 187
Alnwick Shrovetide Football Match, 26
Antient Scorton Silver Arrow, 76
Appleby Horse Fair, 86
Berwick Curfew Run, 107
Burning of Bartle, 113
Castleton Garland Day, 72
Egremont Crab Fair, 142
Grasmere Rushbearing, 98
Kettlewell Scarecrow Festival, 116
Marsden Cuckoo Day, 31
Marsden Imbolc Fire Festival, 210
Moulton Crow Fair, 106
Pace Egging Plays, 34
Ringing the Devil's Knell, 172
Slaithwaite Moonraking, 213
Sowerby Bridge Rushbearing, 136
St Wilfrid's Feast Procession, 107
Whalton Baal Fire, 94
Whitby Penny Hedge, 52
World Coal Carrying Championships, 31

East England

Colne Oyster Fisheries Opening Ceremony, 134
Ely Eel Day, 49
Maldon Mud Race, 76
Whittlesea Straw Bear Festival, 202
World Peashooting Championship, 100

The Midlands

Abbots Bromley Horn Dance, 140
Hare Pie Scramble and Bottle Kicking, 32
Haxey Hood, 194
Tissington Well Dressing, 54

Southeast England

Bampton Morris Dance, 66
Beating the Bounds, 56
Boar's Head Ceremony, 216
Bramble Bank Cricket Match, 126
Braughing Old Man's Day, 144
Bread Ahead Lammas Day, 108
British and World Marbles Championship, 30
Easter Monday Lifting, 30
Eton Wall Game, 160
Grimaldi Clown Service, 213
Hastings Jack in the Green, 44
High Wycombe Mayor Weigh-In, 58
Hungerford Hocktide, 36
Hunting the Mallard, 212
Knighthood of the Old Green, 118
Lewes Bonfire, 150
London Pickle Festival, 158
Mary Gibson's Mausoleum Inspection, 112
Mayor of Ock Street, 84
Olney Pancake Race, 24
Oxford University Tortoise Race, 48
St Bartholomew's Bun Race, 117
Swan Upping, 102
Twelfth Night, 190

Southwest England

Blackawton International Festival of Worm Charming, 46
Burning the Ashen Faggot, 198
Cooper's Hill Cheese-Rolling, 60
Crying the Neck, 130
Glastonbury Festival, 86
Great Wishford's Oak Apple Day, 74
Helston Flora Day, 50
Holy Thorn Cutting, 164
The Hunting of the Earl of Rone, 68
Hurling the Silver Ball, 214
Marldon Apple Pie Fair, 138
Montol, 166
Old Time Paper Boys, 177
Ottery St Mary Tar Barrels, 154
Padstow Obby Oss, 40
Punkie Night, 146
Randwick Wap, 49
Robert Dover's Olimpick Games, 70
Tetbury Woolsack Races, 64
Tom Bawcock's Eve, 170
Turning the Stone, 156
World Nettle Eating Championship, 92

Various Locations

Samhain and Halloween, 148
Summer Solstice, 88
Sword Dancing, 180
Wassailing, 182

Folk Britain:
A Guide for Modern Times
First edition, first printing

Published in 2026 by
Hoxton Mini Press, London

Text by Tom Howells
Editing by Olivia Kumar
& Florence Ward
Design & production by Dom Grant
Production control by David Brimble
Proofreading by Gaynor Sermon
Editorial support by Emma Seckel
& Kate Overy
Interior illustrations by Jen Ament

Thank you to all of the individuals and institutions who have provided images and arranged permissions. While every effort has been made to trace the present copyright holders, we apologise in advance for any unintentional omission or error, and would be pleased to insert the appropriate acknowledgement in any subsequent edition.

A CIP catalogue record for this book is available from the British Library.

ISBN: 978-1-917719-44-5

Printed and bound by
OZGraf, Poland

Manufacturer: Hoxton Mini Press,
104 Northside Studios, 16–29
Andrews Road, London, E8 4QF
www.hoxtonminipress.com

Represented by: Authorised
Rep Compliance Ltd., Ground
Floor, 71 Lower Baggot Street,
Dublin, D02 P593, Ireland
www.arccompliance.com

Hoxton Mini Press is an environmentally conscious publisher, committed to offsetting our carbon footprint. This book is 100 per cent carbon compensated, with offset purchased from Stand For Trees.

Every time you order from our website, we plant a tree:
www.hoxtonminipress.com

FSC
www.fsc.org
MIX
Paper | Supporting responsible forestry
FSC® C163799